Cinema Between Media

An Intermediality Approach

Jørgen Bruhn and Anne Gjelsvik

EDINBURGH
University Press

Edinburgh University Press is one of the leading university presses in the UK. We publish academic books and journals in our selected subject areas across the humanities and social sciences, combining cutting-edge scholarship with high editorial and production values to produce academic works of lasting importance. For more information visit our website: edinburghuniversitypress.com

Edinburgh University Press Ltd
The Tun – Holyrood Road
12 (2f) Jackson's Entry
Edinburgh EH8 8PJ

Typeset in 10.5/12pt Janson by
Servis Filmsetting Ltd, Stockport, Cheshire, and
printed and bound in Great Britain

A CIP record for this book is available from the British Library

ISBN 978 1 4744 2901 6 (hardback)
ISBN 978 1 4744 2902 3 (paperback)
ISBN 978 1 4744 2903 0 (webready PDF)
ISBN 978 1 4744 2904 7 (epub)

Figures image credits
1.1–1.4 © Warner Brothers; 2.1 © RKO; 4.1–4.6 © Motlys; 5.1–5.4 © Final Cut Productions; 6.1–6.8 © Werc Werk Works & Telling Pictures; 7.1–7.2 © Columbia Pictures; 7.3 © Pete Souza/The White House; 7.4 © Richard Drew; 7.5–7.7 © Columbia Pictures; 8.1–8.2 © Eskwad Production; 8.3–8.5 © Exposure Productions; 8.6 © James Balog

Contents

Preface and Acknowledgements

For some years now, we have been studying and teaching intermediality, film studies, narrative theory, and neighbouring subjects; and for some time we have written articles and given presentations, individually or together, on these and related matters. At a certain point, we agreed to collect some of our thoughts on intermediality and cinema in a more well-organised and substantial form – a form that would eventually become this volume.

As we will note a few times in the following pages, the basic idea behind this book is to attempt to merge two fields of study that have not been sufficiently linked and related thus far: the field of intermedial studies and the field of film theory and analysis. We hope we have found a way of doing so in this book, which is directed towards students (in the widest sense of the word) of film who are looking for useful new ways of understanding narrative cinema – be that conventional mainstream cinema, documentary, or art house cinema.

Time will tell if our method will succeed in offering others a richer and more rewarding understanding of cinema but, at the very least, we have ourselves taken pleasure in developing this analytical and theoretical methodology, and we find the practical application of it very worthwhile. Aspects of our methodological suggestions and theoretical arguments can certainly be criticised, and parts of them probably need reformulation or rethinking by students, colleagues, or film buffs around the world. This is exactly the kind of conversation we hope to open with this book, and we welcome any future discussions sparked by our thoughts. We are certain that such dialogue will be fruitful and even necessary to the fields of both intermedial studies and film studies.

We are each aware that we could not have written this book alone; this is why we decided to join forces in the first place. But besides understanding and praising the gifts and possibilities of co-writing, we need to mention a number of smart and critical colleagues who offered invaluable feedback on different drafts of our chapters. Marta Eidsvåg, Dag Sødtholdt, Lars Elleström, Eirik Frisvold Hanssen, Ágnes Pethő, Niklas Salmose, Sara Brinch, and Henriette Thune have all contributed insightful comments on individual chapters of the book: Thank you. A few of the chapters have been discussed at seminars at the Centre for

Intermedial and Multimodal research centre in Växjö, which gave us many important ideas and perspectives. Chapter 7, which is on *Zero Dark Thirty*, benefited from a discussion at the Face of Terror workshop in Trondheim in September 2017. Concerning the chapter on climate change documentaries, we want to give a warm thank you to Master of climate science Torr Cumming, who published an article on this subject with Anne Gjelsvik, but agreed to let the ideas be rethought in an intermedial direction. Also, we want to thank the anonymous reviewers at Edinburgh University Press who gave many helpful suggestions and critiques. Last but not least we will thank Gillian Leslie for her enthusiasm and support for this book from the very first day that we approached her with the idea.

Earlier versions of some of the chapters have previously been published in *Journal of Scandinavian Cinema* 4/2012, (Chapter 5), *Word and Image* 4/2014 (Chapter 6), *Ekfrase* 6/2016 (Chapter 8, Anne Gjelsvik and Torr Cumming).

1 Introduction: Cinema Between Media

In the second half of the nineteenth century, several different technological apparatuses for reproducing the external world were invented. Many words were used to describe these new devices – such as Kinetoscope or Theatrograph – created to show moving pictures to audiences.[1] As a result of inventions such as these, artists found new ways to narrate stories and reflect the world. In the following, we will call these inventions, created to record and project moving images, 'cinema'. Step by step, these technologies and traditions became part of an art form,[2] but as one of the newest of the arts, it has often been described as an art form *between media*. This is the starting point for our book, *Cinema Between Media*.

As cinema shares its basic material with photography (the exposure of an image on photographic film) it has sometimes been described as a mechanical, direct reproduction of reality, but early cinema borrowed heavily from traditional performing arts, like theatre, vaudeville, and tableau vivant. Narrative forms of literature, particularly the novel, have also played important roles in shaping narrative cinema. The list of influencing forms goes on, and includes music, opera, magic, architecture, photography and painting; and following the recent historical advents of technical media such as the VCR and the DVD, and the importance of the digitalisation of the medium, the notion of cinema as a mixed medium has become even more prominent within film theory. In other words: cinema is currently and always has been intermedial.

However, it could be argued that the acknowledgement of this has not had enough of an impact on the practice of academic film analysis. One reason for this is that theorists and critics have been more occupied with discussions of what cinema is (and can be) in distinction to other art forms. Accordingly, our aim in this book is to rethink the practice of film analysis, using concepts and analytical tools derived mainly from the fields of media theory and intermediality. An important exception to film scholars' lack of interest in intermedial theory has been Ágnes Pethő, who in her book *Cinema and Intermediality: the passion for the in-between* (2011) provides a valuable history of the methodological questions concerning film and intermediality, and also offers several examples of specific intermedial film analyses. The major difference between our attempt at combining the fields of cinema and intermedial studies (which we describe below) and her work is that we are eager to provide a relatively hands-on repeatable methodology, whereas Pethő develops a more historical and philosophical argument (Pethő 2011).

What happens if we understand cinema as a mixed medium? How should one approach film analysis from an intermedial perspective? What thematic and formal traits will become clear when we look at film as a mixed mediality? These are some of the questions we aim to answer in *Cinema Between Media.*

This volume is primarily intended for higher-level students at universities and colleges, but we also hope film scholars as well as others interested in film analysis may be inspired by our efforts. In order to answer the questions outlined above, we will in this Introduction present the major analytical concepts we find necessary to building a bridge between intermediality theory and film analysis. To demonstrate the value of our theory and our three-step methodology, presented below, and to offer hands-on suggestions for how to conduct intermedial analyses of narrative cinema, we provide seven case studies after this initial chapter (in the last case study we discuss two documentaries). The cases chosen will be presented towards the end of this chapter; their purpose is primarily to exemplify our method, and as such they are not comprehensive or representative, but we hope to offer new and interesting insights to the films. The cases are, however, not representative for contemporary cinema, or for cinema as such, neither in terms of historical representation and geographical breadth nor cinematic genres, but they should nonetheless cover a fairly wide spectrum of narrative cinema.

Generally, we hope that readers will begin with the Introduction and then move on to the case studies, but we have tried to write each case study in a style and form that makes it accessible even to readers who have browsed only casually through the terminological and methodological arguments of this chapter. Our suggested methodology follows a sequential structure that we hope is illuminating and easy to follow. However, there are certainly other ways of conducting intermedial film analysis, and there will be a certain formal variation in our chapters; some chapters follow the methodology step by step, others move more freely through their analysis. We hope our way of working can be inspirational also to those who might choose to structure their analyses differently.

1.1 The case study

We apply this analytical method to specific films we regard as relatively autonomous entities – despite the fact that the notion of the autonomous work has been criticised and deconstructed more than once. Susan Sontag's influential essay 'Against Interpretation' generated a big discussion about the role case studies can play in art criticism, and the relationship between content and form (Sontag 1966). Our aim is that our model will show how form and content are closely related. Mieke Bal, among many others, has also observed that 'the case study has acquired a dubious reputation as a facile entrance into theoretical generalization and speculation' (Bal 2010), and one does run two obvious risks when using singular works as case studies: the critic might 'cherry-pick' works that all too easily exemplify some preconceived ideas, or the case studies may end up illustrating nothing but atomistic, isolated insights that cannot be generalised. We find, actually, that our cases often encourage us to stretch both our methodological approach and the theoretical terms, and put pressure on the three-step model we suggest. This is not, we believe, a sign that our model or methodology in general ought to be skipped; rather, it shows the limits of any interpretative method when confronted with artistic material. In addition, we think that a good case study can give insight to the film, the method and even contribute to the development of theory.

What does intermediality mean for cinema studies?

The scholarly study of 'media' or 'intermediality' encompasses broad fields and has a long history that emerged from an interest in inter-aesthetic (often called 'inter-art' phenomena) and analytical methods. The term intermediality has gained popularity and influence despite the sometimes disconcerting confusion about whether intermediality is an *object* of study, a *method* of study, or a *theory* about a category of objects. In this book, we will approach all of these categories, but we aim to be clear about what level we work on, as well as the 'kind' of intermediality in question.

Intermedial studies is often used synonymously with inter-aesthetic research or 'interart' studies. Compared to 'interart' studies, the term intermediality designates a broader aesthetical and technological field of investigation. Instead of focusing only on the conventional arts (music, fine art, literature), intermedial studies open the investigation up to other contemporary aesthetic forms such as performance art, digital poetry, non-artistic medialities such as advertising, political campaigns, or mass media content – and, of course, film.[3] Furthermore, as our case studies will demonstrate, non-aesthetic, everyday media such as computers, telephones or newspapers may also play important roles in the analyses.

Although intermedial studies is better suited to cover the entire field than interart studies, reservations have been raised concerning the term. Intermediality seems to imply that the object of study is relations 'between' (*inter*) media or medialities. The prefix 'inter' restricts the object of study to a specific, limited group of media products, as opposed to 'normal', 'pure', or 'monomedial' phenomena, that is, media products that do not move between medialities or cross any mediality borders. Consequently, the term seems to apply to a relationship between (*inter*) texts or medialities, rather than express that a merging of media is occurring within a single medium or artefact (Bruhn 2016, 2010a).

The point of departure for this book is that all specific media products and medialities, including cinema, inevitably are mixed constellations. We will argue that there is no such thing as autonomous or pure medialities. The idea that cinema is a mixed medium is of course not new, but other perspectives have dominated the discourse in film studies. The conventions that make us think about media (or art forms) as distinct forms separated from each other are the result of media history, the history of media theories and, not least, the history of academia. When cinema became an academic discipline in the 1960s, film scholars, although drawing on other disciplines such as philosophy, literary theory, and anthropology, sought to differentiate the new discipline from older ones.

Even earlier, at the beginning of the twentieth century when cinema itself was a new-born medium, film theorists foregrounded the uniqueness of the medium when arguing that it should be considered art proper. Accordingly, an important early goal for film scholars was to find the essence of the new art form (Andrew 1976). Thus, cinema has been described as motion pictures or moving images, based on photographic technology (for most of cinema history film was on celluloid, today most films are digital). The visual focus and the illusion of movement are often the starting points for scholarly books about the cinematic medium (Bordwell and Thompson 2017).

Typically for the focus on cinema as a visual media, the current Wikipedia definition of cinema reads as follows: 'A film, also called a movie, motion picture, theatrical film or photoplay, is a series of still images which, when shown on a screen, creates the illusion of moving images' (for another brief definition, see our opening to Chapter 7). Of course, it is common knowledge that cinema is more than its moving images; it is by now convention in introductions to film analysis to describe cinema as a medium based on four major categories: *mise en scène*, cinematography, editing, and sound (Bordwell and Thompson 2017, Corrigan and Barry 2012). The emphasis on cinema as an *audio*-visual medium has also been strengthened over the last decades, with Rick Altman and composer and film theorist Michel Chion's *Audio-vision: Sound on Screen* (1994) as central contributors to the field (Altman 1992, 1980; Chion 1994). Chion argues that rather than see images and hear sounds separately when we encounter cinema, we perceive both elements together, and that what we interpret as rhythm, for instance, is a mixture of sound, editing and camera movements (Chion 1994). Chion has also discussed voice in cinema, but despite him and others arguing for more attention to sound (music and sound effects) the visual elements of film still receive the most attention. The visual versus verbal divide has been discussed and criticised in books such as Kamilla Elliott's *Rethinking the Novel/Film Debate* (with special focus on the problem of adaptation studies) and Sarah Kozloff's book *Overhearing Film Dialogue* (Elliott 2003; Kozloff 2000). Although Elliott shows that novels can be visual and films verbal, and Kozloff demonstrates how to analyse the use of dialogue in narrative film, the verbal element of film is still often both overheard and overlooked.

When Bordwell and Thompson analyse the use and function of sound in film, they investigate the perceptual properties of sound (loudness, pitch, timbre), dimensions of film sound (rhythm, time, space, etc.) and discuss the difference between diegetic and non-diegetic sound, but they do not pay much attention to dialogue, although the focus on sound has been strengthened in the latest edition of *Film Art* (Bordwell and Thompson 2017). Most of the films we watch are filled with dialogue and/or other verbal elements, but close attention to this cinematic device is usually only given when words have a particularly important position in the film, e.g. *My Dinner with Andre*, Louis Malle (1981), where the whole film is a conversation at a dinner table, or are pivotal in the narrative, e.g. Denis Villeneuve's *Arrival* from 2016, a science-fiction film based on a short story by Ted Chiang, which is all about language and communication. But we are often faced with the argument that dialogue or a speech in a film is too 'literary', and that, consequently, the use of voice-over is un-cinematic. However, the way characters talk in films is a result of conventions, historical changes, and influence from other media. Theatre, novels, and then later radio, helped cinema in 'finding its own voice' (Leitch 2013).

Classical film theorists would praise cinema's ability to capture reality (André Bazin, Siegfried Kracauer), create new meaning through montage (Sergej Eisenstein), move in time and space (Hugo Münsterberg), and thus stress its differences from painting, theatre or literature (Andrew 1976; Elsaesser and Hagener 2009). Such medium specificity claims – that there is something film can do or represent that other art forms cannot – have generated a lot of debate both within film studies and in neighbouring disciplines, such as adaptation studies.[4] While some scholars are in favour of studying film by foregrounding what they see as medium specificity, others argue against what they call medium essentialism. This is the idea that each art form or medium has distinctive traits that distinguishes it from other art forms and medialities (Carroll 1996).

The discussion about mixed versus pure art forms has a much longer history than film and film theory. The concept of *paragone* (roughly corresponding to 'comparison'), originates in Renaissance art theory and relates to a ranking competition among the arts – each form vying to be deemed the best and most valuable. Famously, Leonardo da Vinci argued that painting was the highest example of artistic form, and this contention was refuted by, among others, Michelangelo, who counter-argued for the primacy of sculpture. The paragone debate has been a perennial discussion in Western cultural history; recently a German collection of essays, inspired by intermedial studies, reinvigorated the idea of the 'competition' between the arts and media by analysing not only the classical art forms, but also television, advertising, graphic novels, and computer games in a framework inspired by the sociology of Pierre Bourdieu (Degner and Wolf 2010). In our book, we will pursue the idea that it is indeed possible to see current competitions among the arts, and to trace a paragone debate in modern media products such as film and television. While cinema was first compared with theatre, and then later with the novel, it should come as no surprise that comparisons between film and television (but also computer games) are predominant in contemporary media criticism.

The complicated history of the blending of medialities and art forms can also be illuminated by looking at the difference between the tradition pointing out the benefits of the meeting and merging of art forms and that which offers warnings about the consequences of such mixing. Utilising terms from widely different periods, we can contrast the Roman writer Horace's dictum 'ut pictura poesis' ('as in painting, so in poetry') with ideas found in G. E. Lessing's eigthteenth-century essay on the monumental Laocoön Group sculpture – an essay subtitled 'On the limits of painting and poetry'.[5] Lessing's interrogation is among the inspirations for some problematic but often repeated 'truths' of aesthetic theory concerning the relations between the arts: such as the claim that literature deals with and represents time, whereas painting should stick to spatial, or non-temporal, presentation. His treatise has inspired numerous debates about medium specificity, either as descriptive formats or as normative dogma, from his own day to the present, across the fields of literature, painting, and film.[6]

The struggle of *ut pictura poesis* versus the Laocoön tradition can be traced back and forth through cultural history, and it can be found in different academic disciplines and art forms (art, music, or literature). Needless to say, there are huge differences in whether these aesthetic ideas are seen as descriptive or prescriptive (or – often – both). Richard Wagner's late Romantic and politically utopian concept of a *Gesamtkunstwerk*, a total work of art, is one version of the *ut pictura* tradition. Several of the so-called historical avant-gardes of the beginning of the twentieth century believed that the mixing of art forms was not only possible, but necessary in order to achieve the highest artistic and political/spiritual goals (Bürger 1984). Ágnes Pethő continues this appraisal of the aesthetic virtues of mixedness and offers stimulating interpretations of a number of modern and postmodern auteurs (Pethő 2011). The numerous attempts at specifying the different art forms (or media), as well as limiting them to their own formal investigation (as in Clement Greenberg's lifelong engagements with Modernist art), led to the influential notion of medium specificity, which can be seen as a twentieth-century version of Lessing's idea of establishing strict formal and normative borders between the arts.

In film theory, such perspectives had many consequences, one of them being the difference between the so-called realist position and the formalist one. This distinction was foregrounded by leading realist film theorists Siegfried Kracauer (1889–1966) and André Bazin (1918–58). In 'The Ontology of the Photographic Image', Bazin argued that 'the indexical nature of the image means that realism is never simple stylistic choice on the part of the filmmaker. Realism, in an important sense, is already there in the image; realism is given' (Bazin 2009a). Whereas the realist position often has been described as seeing cinema as a window, the formalist position sees it as a frame (Andrew 1976:12; Elsaesser and Hagener, 2009). These metaphors suggest different qualities in cinema as 'one looks *through* a window, but one looks *at* a frame', and where the window ideally becomes invisible and makes cinema look real, the frame draws attention to cinema as something artificial (Elsasesser and Hagener 2009: 14–15; see also Friedberg 2006 for interesting perspectives on these traditions). When discussing the basic elements of the film medium, Rudolf Arnheim (1904–2007) foregrounded how cinema created a world of its own, distinct from the physical world, due to film's lack of colour and three-dimensional depth, and the margins of the frame (Arnheim 1958). Accordingly, filmmakers should pursue, in Arnheim's opinion, the elements that distinguish film not only from other arts, but from life itself, and for that reason Arnheim was in favour of black and white silent films throughout his life. Such normative positions are not only found among theorists; filmmakers have also voiced their opinions about the specificity of the medium, such as when Ingmar Bergman describes Russian director Andrej Tarkovsky as 'the one who invented a *new language*, true to the nature of film, as it captures life as a reflection, life as a dream' (Gianvito 2006).

Such differing views of what cinema is, can do, or should be, have also led to different approaches to *what* to study when analysing films: the sound (Michel Chion), the movement (Tom Gunning), the close-up (Bela Balázs), et cetera (Chion 1994, Gunning 2008, Balázs 1924). We will also investigate what cinematic elements do, for instance the role of sound or motion in a film or a scene, and we will argue that the inherent medial mixedness, or what we could term the 'heteromedial' aspect of film, is a major characteristic. As suggested above, the term heteromediality has some benefits over the more common 'intermediality' (Bruhn 2010). Heteromediality (hetero: other, or mixed) emphasises that blending is an a priori condition in all media products and medialities, and that the blending aspects consequently do not constitute a peripheral phenomenon or a marginal subgroup: mixedness characterises all medialities and all specific media products. Mixedness comes first, so to speak; the supposed monomedial purity of any specific medial object is the result of an active purification, rather than the other way round (Bruhn 2010, 2016).

This, we claim, could be the central starting point for the intermedial study of cinema – all cinematic texts are medially mixed, but in infinitely differentiated ways and to different effects and meanings. In the following, 'heteromediality' signifies the general, a priori condition of mixedness, whereas we employ 'intermediality' when discussing more specific analytical questions.

What does media mean?

But what exactly are these media that can be mixed, or rather, whose very nature it is to be mixed? Historically, most discussions within intermedial studies have employed the concept medium/media, but the term is much-debated. Central media studies scholar Werner Wolf notes ironically that '[c]uriously, problems of definition and typology have not hindered intermediality research. The most obvious among these is the problem of defining 'medium' itself' (Wolf 2005).

One solution – which has been employed more or less consistently throughout this introductory chapter – is to use the more open form mediality/medialities instead (Wolf 2008, Mitchell and Hansen 2010). In Mitchell and Hansen's anthology *Critical Terms for Media Studies*, 'mediation' plays an important role in changing the question of what a medium *is* towards one of what media *do* – in other words what the process of mediation involves. Mitchell and Hansen showed that mediation, unlike the objectified existence of a medium/media, is an activity – the process of mediating – which per definition also includes a media product. These are some of the reasons why, in this book, instead of the term 'medium' (with the implied conceptual connotations of objecthood), we suggest 'mediality' and 'medialities' (plural), which relate to the process of mediation in communicative situations. However, as the reader might have noticed, we do at times use medium/media and mediality/medialities interchangeably – this is done in order to achieve variation, or when 'medialities' feels particularly clumsy.

When it comes to a working definition and stratification of the concept of medialities, we find that Lars Elleström's theorisation offers a precise but relatively flexible definition of mediality as a mixture of media and modalities (Elleström 2010b, 2014). Elleström has ventured to combine two often overlapping theoretical frameworks: intermediality and multimodality studies. These are two traditions that, each often without acknowledging the respective achievements of the other, work from more or less the same assumptions, namely that all communicative action takes place by way of devices that mix media (often understood as communicative channels or art forms) or modalities (often understood as more basic aspects of communicative action, such as sound, images or other sensual signs). By means of Elleström's cross-fertilisation of intermedial studies and multimodality/social semiotics, it becomes possible to construct an understanding of how all media are really modally mixed – and consequently that there is no such thing as a monomedial or 'monomodal' communicative situation or media product – which is another way of arguing for the heteromedial condition of all communication.

What is particularly useful in Elleström's model is that it offers a much needed clarification of the many different notions of medium that are available and in use in everyday talk, as well as in academic discussions and cultural criticism. A mobile phone, a Klee oil painting, a television set, and the genre of opera may all in given contexts exemplify 'medium'. Elleström however defines medium using a model consisting of a *basic*, a *qualified*, and a *technical* media dimension. The main idea is that what we normally call a medium, or perhaps an art form, needs to be broken down into three interrelated dimensions that are often confused and conflated: *basic media*, *qualified media*, and *technical media.*

The *basic* media dimension may be exemplified by written words, moving images, or rhythmic sound patterns. These particular basic media dimensions may, under certain conditions, be part of *qualified* media, such as narrative written literature, a newspaper article, a documentary film, or symphonic music. Thus, qualified media in the arts are more or less synonymous with what is often referred to as art forms. Cinema, written narrative literature, and sculpture are examples of qualified media, but not all qualified media are aesthetic. We also find qualified media outside the arts, in areas such as the verbal language of the sports page in newspapers, advertising jingles, or in the non-aesthetic verbal language of legal prose. The third media component, *technical* media, is the material-technological dimension, which makes qualified media perceptible in the first place, say, a TV screen, a piece of paper, or a mobile phone interface. In short, technical media *display* basic or qualified media.

This division of all media products into three media dimensions makes it possible to include anything from the mobile phone interface to a Renaissance poem into the investigation of medialities (the first being a technical medium, the second an example of the qualified medium of written literature), but it also enables us to differentiate between them in analytical terms. The qualified medium of cinema accordingly consists of basic media like moving images, words, music etc., and can be watched (and heard) on technical media such as a computer, a television screen or the display of a mobile phone. Throughout our case studies, we will hopefully demonstrate the usefulness of these distinctions.

Following this way of understanding medialities, any media product (in its three dimensions) enables communication, but this positive understanding of medialities is not the only way to understand communication. It is useful to remember that communication has historically been understood in two, fundamentally different ways and thus two ways of understanding the function of medialities in communication.[7]

One strong, but also heterogeneous tradition, beginning with Plato's *Phaedrus*, is suspicious and even fearful toward any mediating objects. In Plato's case, writing was the new medium that threatened both authentic communication and the human being's ability to use memory as the major storage medium. But in subsequent historical contexts, this anxiety came to relate to all imaginable medialities that threatened to interfere with the face-to-face dialogue between speaker and interlocutor, sender and receiver. This tradition of understanding media in communication as an estranging and destructive threat to authentic co-presence and deep, mutual understanding, will be referred to as the 'mediaphobic' position from here on. John Durham Peters – and we follow him – is highly critical of this tendency, because it tends to idealise face-to-face presence as the only legitimate communicative relation:

> The image of two speakers taking turns in order to move progressively toward fuller understanding of each other masks two deeper facts: that all discourse, however many the speakers, must bridge the gap between one turn and the next, and that the intended addressee may never be identical with the actual one.
>
> (Peters 1999)

As an alternative to this face-to-face dialogue-model, which often implicates a communication magically unfettered by any medialities, Durham Peters demonstrates that a notion of communication as dissemination is a much more fruitful model for how communication works. For our purposes this model is interesting because it does not exclude or ban medialities.

Communication-as-dissemination implies a fundamental *distance* between sender and receiver, and it is this distance that implies the necessity of the presence of medialities: medialities *create* communication, they do not disturb it. The idea of communication as dissemination entails real bodies sending open-ended signs, by way of material medialities, to whoever wants to interpret them – be it the person next to you on the train, the reader of a book, a radio programme listener, or the participant in a social medium like Facebook. This is a much more realistic and indeed attractive understanding of all the communicative aspects of people's lives, which we, in contradistinction to the suspicious 'mediaphobic' position, will call the 'mediaphile' position. This dichotomy between a friendly or a hostile stance towards the function of media will pop up as a theme in some of our case studies.

Combination or transformation

The problem of describing the mixed media of cinema may be simplified by dividing the heteromediality of cinema into two dimensions: one consisting of a process of *transformation* and another of the phenomenon of *combination.*

Transformation concerns the medial content or form, which in a temporal process is transformed from one medium to another. Adaptation studies, for instance the study of the transport from novels to film, is one particular investigation of an extremely broad phenomenon. Allen Ginsberg's poem *Howl*, parts of which are transformed into the film *Howl* (see Chapter 6), is an example of this. In the film, the transformation takes place when the poem written on paper is being read out loud, when the poem is being partly reproduced on written pages in the film, and when it is being represented in court as a printed book.

Combination aspects, on the other hand, concern phenomena where two or more medial form aspects co-exist in the same medium at the same time – for instance when a Cézanne painting is represented in a film(*Howl*) accompanied by jazz music. These two dimensions of intermediality are not mutually exclusive, and in our analysis, we shall alternate between seeing specific fragments as part of a transformational change *and* as part of the combination of media in the film.

The transformation per definition contains a temporal perspective. First, there is a play, then it is turned into a film; first there is a film, then it is turned into an amusement park; first there is a painting, then there is a poem representing this painting, etc. Computer games are made into films (*Assassins Creed* 2016) and films are made into computer games (*Ice Age* 2002). In this large corpus, introduced and discussed in Linda Hutcheon's *A Theory of Adaptation* (Hutcheon 2006; see also Bruhn, Gjelsvik, and Hanssen 2013), the medial mix lies, so to speak, in the procedure: certain aspects of the novel (typically: themes, parts of the plot, certain characters, setting etc.) are transported into a film, but certain aspects of the adapted work are necessarily left out or changed beyond recognition. The process is transferring certain aspects while also transforming everything into a new media product (and a different technical medium). A lot of films are based on such transformations, in contemporary media culture the typical process being a bestselling novel or series of comic books turned into a Hollywood film. Notable examples are the many films based on the Marvel universe, the direct adaptation of the *Hunger Games* books, the comprehensive *Harry Potter* franchises or the television series *Game of Thrones.*

In the other large group, we have the combination of otherwise distinct medialities inside the same media product: in a pop song, the verbal, sung text is combined with music; on a Facebook page, photographs are combined with text and graphic design; on a poster, images exist side by side with words. In this group, aspects of different medialities exist synchronously, as opposed to the temporal process of transformation in the first group. In cinema, this is obvious but rarely made explicit. A film often (not always) starts with verbal and aural information, such as the name of the production company and music, before any other imagery appears (see Chapter 7 on *Zero Dark Thirty*). Images can be animated, or photographed, moving or still. Through the film, visual and verbal elements will be combined in a multitude of different ways, from the production company's name visualised in their logo, the voice-over accompanying images of a landscape or the dialogue between two actors visible on the screen.

From an analytical point of view, it is helpful to divide all medialities into 'temporal transformation' or 'synchronous combination', but it should not be forgotten that such a distinction is pragmatic rather than essential. Given the condition that all medialities are mixed, it follows, on one hand, that all media products are in fact a combination of mediality aspects. Given the fundamental idea of intertextuality (which states that all texts are versions of earlier texts), on the other hand, we may conclude that all medialities are, basically, the result of a transformation.

Consequently, when performing a medial analysis on a specific film, one might investigate either mixtures (combination) or traces (transformation), and thus the film, from a medial perspective, is comparable to the famous duck-rabbit illusion: depending on analytical interest, you can choose to perceive a media product as either a combination *or* a process of transformation; both dimensions are inherent aspects of the specific film. To get the fullest possible description and interpretation, one might combine the two approaches, but many specific analyses will typically focus on one of the two aspects. In our analysis of Epstein and Friedman's curiously mixed biopic adaptation of Allen Ginsberg's *Howl*, for instance, we hardly go into the adaptation analysis, and discuss instead the formal as well as the more philosophical questions relating to the combination axis.

Intermedial reference, formal imitation, medial projection

Further useful distinctions are 'intermedial reference', 'formal imitation', and 'medial projection', all of which are parts of the media transformation perspective previously mentioned. A first distinction is that between intermedial reference and formal imitation. The creator of a film may, consciously or unconsciously, evoke or insert a medial reference to another real or fictional media product. In *Louder Than Bombs*, there is a reference to an earlier film that Gabriel Byrne acted in, which also plays a small part in the narrative (making this an intramedial reference, because the source and target media are identical). In *Howl*, we see an LP cover in Allen Ginsberg's working room that contributes to establishing a setting and a mood, a typical 'reality effect' (Barthes 1986) that helps create realistic apprehensions of the fictional text (Pethő 2011).

But a media product, or parts of it, can also be formed entirely by mimicking the formal attributes of another mediality. In such cases, we talk about a formal imitation (Wolf 2008, 2011). There are no absolute boundaries between reference versus formal imitation, but a rule of thumb could be that if we are dealing with a specific reference of a media product, the particular example is interchangeable: in *Louder Than Bombs*, for example, we do not necessarily need to know the origin and context of the embarrassing film clip with Gabriel Byrne, it could be any film with the young actor; in *Howl*, the record sleeve could have been any classical composer and the effect of the presence of the music would not change. On the other hand, we could say that formal imitation is what happens in *Girl with a Pearl Earring* (Peter Webber 2003). The film is an adaptation of a novel by Tracy Chevalier (1999) in which Johannes Vermeer's famous painting is described verbally (as an ekphrasis) and plays a crucial role (see Leitch 2009). In the film, we find a visual re-enactment that could be considered as a cinematic ekphrasis (Brinch 2006). Vermeer, who was famous for his sophisticated use of light, inspired the filmmakers to use different film stock and special lighting, in order to capture the style and feeling of the painting. Hollywood star Scarlett Johansson poses as the girl in the painting, in an image that at first glance looks like the original. A more radical example of formal imitation of a painting is found in *Mill and the Cross* (Lech Majewski 2011), where numerous details and some (of a total of 500) characters in Pieter Bruegel the Elder's allegorical painting *The Procession to Calvary* (1564) are brought to life. The painting is recreated as film via special effects, live action, and a large copy of the painting; this is what Pethő would call 'a post-cinematic cross-breed between cinema and painting and installation art' (Pethő 2013).[8] As John Berger demonstrated in his famous television series *Ways of Seeing* (1972), Breughel's painting is so rich in detail that it is easy to move around and focus on different elements, and this is exactly what Majewski does in his adaptation, but the result is a film with much less emphasis on the narrative than we are used to in mainstream cinema.

Seeing the world as if it were a painting has been theorised under the term 'iconic projection', by Swedish scholar Hans Lund (Lund 1992, Tornborg 2014). However, a broader understanding of this mechanism is needed, and 'medial projection' has been proposed (Bruhn 2016), a term which may encompass a much wider array of medial phenomena. Perceiving and describing particular aspects of the world as if it were, or could have been, either a qualified mediality (like music or more specifically a symphony), or a technical mediality (a TV-screen, a canvas), is a common literary device, and actually an intermedial phenomenon. In Mike Leigh's *Mr Turner* (2014), for example, many shots appear to be partly through the eyes of the painter J. M.W. Turner, and are also framed in the same way as the paintings themselves are framed. Medial projection plays a certain role in our analyses, and it is crucial to our attempt to establish a general intermedial analytical model for analysing cinema.

To briefly summarise the arguments so far, we can start by reminding the reader that we define medialities as a broad term consisting of the three internally interrelated dimensions of basic medium, technical medium and qualified medium. We use mediality and media interchangeably in our book. We also made a provisional distinction between medial combination and medial transformation, and mediality reference versus formal imitation, and finally introduced medial projection as yet another way that cinematic texts come in close contact with other aesthetic or non-aesthetic medialities. In the following, we want to propose a methodology for analysing cinema based on these theoretical and analytical terms.

The three-step mediality analysis of film: catalogue, structure, context

The specific methodology we propose is a three-step approach moving from constructing a list of mediality presences, via an examination and structuring of this list (still staying inside the borders of the analysed film) and into an interpretation of the work, often but not always by way of a contextualisation beyond and outside the given film.[9]

1.2 Mediality as motif

We analyse cinematic texts by cataloguing, structuring and contextualising medialities. But how can this method be characterised according to some of the well-known options in film studies and aesthetic analysis? Is it a thematic analysis where the continuous and repeated representation of medialities adds up to an over-arching theme? Not quite; in particular because we tend to focus on the formal importance of the presence and function of medialities as opposed to a content-oriented, thematic analysis. Are medialities, instead, to be understood as a 'leitmotif' in the films we discuss, so that the repeated presence of singular medialities tries to communicate some kind of higher psychological, existential or aesthetic vision? Given the heterogeneous nature of the different medialities, this is not really fitting either.

A better, if somewhat broad description might be to say that we investigate 'mediality as motif', in a broad sense of the word. Bordwell and Thompson describe motif as part of cinema's essential dialectic between repetition and variation:

> *A motif is any significant repeated element that contributes to the overall form*. It may be an object, a color, a place, a person, a sound, or even a character trait.
>
> (Bordwell and Thompson 2017)

Working with a broad notion of medialities (as defined above) it makes sense to say that we investigate medialities as motif; a motif that produces meaning on several levels simultaneously and that, when analysed, becomes part of an overall interpretation of our films.

The repeatable structure of the method is supposed to be sufficiently open to improvisation and creativity to make it useful when analysing the complexities of specific cinematic texts. The methodology does not offer a simple, universal solution for anyone engaging with film studies: we presuppose certain skills in cultural analysis from our reader and are well aware that while in particular the first step is relatively easy to conduct, the second and third steps demand a certain amount of creativity and analytical training and practising.

The first step consists of a fairly loose localisation and cataloguing of the representations of media products, types and aspects in the film. Once again it is important to stress that the focus for us here is the representation of medialities in cinema, rather than readings of cinema as material objects, or understanding the distribution and production of cinema. This first step is intended to generate a *catalogue* of medially interesting phenomena in the analysed film. In this opening phase, we suggest employing as broad a concept of medialities as possible (following the generous definition by Elleström presented above) and registering a large number of aspects connected directly or indirectly to any mediating devices in communicative situations.

Let us demonstrate how the first step in such an analysis (albeit not a fully-fledged analysis) could work with a rather long example. We have chosen the title sequence from Guy Ritchie's *Sherlock Holmes* (2009) as a useful exemplary case.[10] Georg Stanitzek and Noelle Aplevich have described a title sequence as a film 'inside the film', and as the cinematic form that makes use of the highest number of cinematic techniques to the fullest extent possible (Stanitzek and Aplevich 2009). The title sequence could also be described as an intermedial example par excellence, since it almost always will be a very direct combination of sound, verbal text, images, animation and more. In the case of *Sherlock Holmes*, the opening title sequence is quite short; it starts with the Warner Brothers (and the other studios') logo redesigned in cobblestones, and rather than a still before the action starts, the logos are included in a moving camera shot (or in fact the CGI illusion of a moving camera). After a short chase, we find Sherlock Holmes (Robert Downey Jr), Dr Watson (Jude Law), and a policeman (Eddie Marsan) standing in a church. We hear a voice say: 'Gentlemen', and the three men turn around; when the photographer shouts 'cheese' (Figure 1.1), the camera goes off and Sherlock hides his face. The next image shows the photograph that was taken, first a blurred version in motion and then the negative, as if the frozen image is meant to show the process of photo developing (Figure 1.2). The final version of the image is on the front page of a newspaper, this time as a drawing (Figure 1.3). Our view is then expanded (through a motion that looks like camera movement) to expose the full newspaper page, with the title of the cover story, 'Scotland Yard catches killer!', and a second title reading: 'Sherlock Holmes aides police'. If we watch the film on a computer or television, we are able to freeze the image and read the newspaper article in *The Penny Illustrated Paper.* The film quickly focuses on the name Sherlock Holmes (the title of the film) (Figure 1.4), and cuts to a new image: The sign on a wall saying Baker Street, N.W. And so, the story begins. Within the short span of twenty seconds, we have been presented with a camera, a photograph (in two different versions), a drawing, a newspaper, including illustrations, an article, and a street sign.

The second part of the title sequence, normally called the end credits, reuses these elements and combines them with writing: an image of a character in the film is frozen and transformed into a drawing, accompanied by the relevant actor's name, appearing as if written by a calligraphic pen on old paper. Members of the cast, photographers, scriptwriters, editors etc., are listed in a similar way. However, here the combination of images and words is closer to the characteristics of the technical medium of the book, an impression strengthened by the effect of rapidly turning pages. Accordingly, viewers may be reminded of old news media, paintings and books when watching this title sequence.

This first step may be characterised, in comparison with the two steps that follow, as the least creative and most rote-like aspect of the analytical labour. Ideally, different readers with different interpretational agendas should be able to agree upon most of the items on this list, but it cannot be generated without any interpretive considerations whatsoever. Even if it may seem like a rather empty exercise, for many students, simply making such a list induces an important recognition: a supposedly homogenic medium such as film includes many, many represented medialities – it just takes a new analytical perspective to notice.

1.3 Presentation of the analytical results

A relevant question is how to present the results of the analysis conducted via the three-step method. This basically involves two questions: How much of the preparational material of the analysis should be included in a presentation, and in what order?

The question of quantity is of paramount importance in the first step of the analysis: in a student's assignment as well as in a published research article, it is quite tedious – and impossible for practical, space reasons – to include all mediality instances in a film. Only in rare cases is it actually manageable to catalogue all instances (of a certain relevance!). However, in most cases, the writer of the analysis could either add a list in an appendix to the running text or, as we will do in our discussions of most of our

Figure 1.1 Figures 1.1–1.4 illustrate the presence of media in film in a short sequence from the opening of *Sherlock Holmes* (2009). Here we see the camera . . .

Figure 1.2 . . . the photograph exposed . . .

Figure 1.3 . . . as a drawing in a newspaper.

Figure 1.4 The film title as read in the newspaper.

case studies, including *Citizen Kane* and *Howl*, reproduce and analyse a fragment of the entire text that can exemplify the larger trend of the film in question. We often find it helpful to reproduce the presence of medialities by analysing either the opening of a film or a single scene or sequence, but the different choices of representation are meant to illustrate the fact that there are several ways of demonstrating or even visualising the presence of medialities.

When it comes to the order in which the results of the three analytical steps are being presented, it is for reasons of clarity preferable, though not strictly necessary, to follow the sequence of catalogue-structure-context/interpretation. This is the main reason why we prefer to talk about steps of the analysis instead of stages or levels, which imply an already fixed order. However, although we generally see no reason why the analytical work would take on one form or structure (concerning quantity and order), while the presentation of the results would adopt another, in the following case studies, we follow the three steps more or less faithfully.

As the second step of the analysis, we suggest that the viewer structure and organise the large and often incoherent material collected and catalogued in step one. From our experience, we know that this second step demands rigour, because it is all too easy to skip ahead into step three's contextualising activities. In step two, the meaningless list is transformed into some kind of comprehensible and coherent structure. In our example case, we could sum up how the technical media (paper or the camera) in the film could be said to reflect the contemporary media history of Conan Doyle's time, when the *Sherlock Holmes* stories were originally written (1887–1900). Or we could reflect on how the use of photography, newspapers, and books draws attention to the fact that this is a film adaptation of classic literature (See Geraghty 2009).

What we focus on could be dependent on the specific elements of a film or the context of the film. In some of our cases, we will discuss one of the historical dichotomies presented above between, for instance, medial mixedness versus medial purity in step two or three. In some cases, we will discuss the paragone tradition of arts competing to be the 'best' art form. Sometimes the film as a whole aesthetic statement can be seen entering such a discussion. In other cases, we find the abstract paragone discussion embodied in a hierarchy of representatives of the various media (a painter versus an author, for instance). Sometimes the paragone may be detectable on the level of style or form, where the director's aesthetic choices may express a schism between a descriptive, 'painterly' style versus a more literary, discursive style.

These dichotomies, or whichever structure we have described in step two, are now ready to be contextualised or, as we often say in the case studies, 'framed' into some larger context, which may fall into numerous different categories. The structures of step two may, in the third step, be related to a biographical context for a filmmaker (for instance Joachim Trier or Jan Troell in Chapters 4 and 5), or more comprehensive aesthetic, theoretical, or art-sociological patterns or formations (as we foreground in Chapter 6 on *Howl*). Of course, the requisite context may also be technological, or an ideological formation in the society in which the film was made, or the society represented in the work (which is the case in our reading of *Zero Dark Thirty*).

If we were to continue our sketch of a possible interpretation of the *Sherlock Holmes* title sequence, a tempting contextualisation would be a comparison between the 1900-ish media situation in Guy Ritchie's film and the 2000-something setting of the BBC's series *Sherlock* (2010–16). In the BBC series, the story has been moved to a contemporary London, and the title sequence starts with a hectic overview of Leicester Square: horses have been replaced with cars, the newspaper with big neon signs. Whereas the film's credit sequence was illustrated with drawings, the BBC series credit sequence is based on time-lapse and tilt-shift technology, which creates the feeling that we as viewers can look down on Sherlock's world from above. The tilt-shift effect can distort perspective and create the feeling that we are looking at a London in miniature (Brinch 2013). In sum, the BBC's title sequence foregrounds the role of mobile phones and surveillance technology. In the first example, the media is watching what Sherlock is doing, but in the BBC version it is less clear who is looking at whom, a change which echoes the change in our mediated environment during this historical period.

As will hopefully become clear in our longer, exploratory case studies in the following chapters, our aim is to show that when focusing on cataloguing and ordering the medialities of a given film, one's attention is almost invariably drawn to larger contexts beyond the question of mediation or representation itself. To put it differently: our method of analysing the media aspects of cinematic texts is a maieutic method; it focuses our attention toward a certain 'dimension' of the text, and thereby offers access to aspects that would otherwise have remained undetected. And we repeat: the maieutic three steps are no guarantee for a productive reading, the student needs to bring engagement and basic analytical skills to the table.

1.4 What not to include

For an example of what *not* to include in a catalogue, let's take the soundtrack of a film. The soundtrack of a film is a complex mixed mediality (consisting of dialogue, music, sound, voice-over) whose function and presence needs to be analysed in any cinematic text. But that does not mean that all instances of the soundtrack in a film should be put on the list (which would mean, basically, that the entire film would be reproduced soundbite for soundbite in the list).

In the *Sherlock Holmes* sequence we focused on the visual elements, but we also mentioned the spoken words. We could have foregrounded the click sound of the camera blitz, and other spectators perhaps would be more interested in the striking theme music composed by Hans Zimmer, allegedly played on an old broken piano, but we chose another analytical perspective in our discussion. So even if the list resulting from the first step is supposed to be constructed in compliance with relatively objective standards, the list is, of course, following pragmatic considerations.

Overview of the book

To summarise, the main approach of this book is to combine intermedial theory with terminology from conventional film analysis. The purpose of this combination is the construction of a model for film analysis that will prove useful in pedagogical settings (film analysis and cultural studies classes, etc.), but also in more theoretical discussions of the form and functions of film and film analysis. The theoretical model will be exemplified in six case studies, covering films where the qualified media – photography, literature (poetry and novel), theatre, music, painting, and animation – are vital components.

We have chosen six of our case studies with the aim of providing a broad (but not comprehensive) overview of important trends in contemporary cinema, while also offering an analysis of Orson Welles's classic film *Citizen Kane*, hinting at a historical background for contemporary cinema's intermedial aesthetics. All of the films discussed are currently in international distribution with English subtitles.

The case studies range from mainstream popular films that would not typically be considered interesting for a formal, intermedial analysis (*Zero Dark Thirty*) to more high-brow films where the other arts clearly occupy the centre stage (*Birdman*). The iconic *Citizen Kane* is meant to offer a certain historical depth to our general argument: the inherent intermediality of cinema is a general condition, and not only a fact of contemporary film. Furthermore, we offer analyses of two films in the borderland between mainstream and independent cinema (*Everlasting Moments* and *Louder Than Bombs*); and a film from the independent/festival sphere (*Howl*) will give us the possibility of discussing an interesting blend of documentary and fiction material, as well as an unusual mix of live-action and animation film.

The chosen films enable the book to move from the 'manifestly' intermedial, in *Citizen Kane* and *Howl*, to the much more 'discreet' intermedial aspects of other films such as *Zero Dark Thirty*. In addition, forms ranging from traditional art, such as music and theatre, to modern media and surveillance technologies are represented.

In Chapter 2, Media Behind the Scenes, we will discuss Orson Welles's classic *Citizen Kane* (1941). This film has regularly been praised as one of the absolute masterpieces in film history, for a number of reasons, including psychological depth, political critique and technological virtuosity. In our analysis, however, we will instead understand the film as a masterpiece of mixed media. As this is the first chapter that employs the three-step analytical model, we will focus particularly on the first step, i.e. the cataloguing of media presence, which is so salient in Welles's film but is mentioned usually only in passing in the rich critical literature concerned with the film. We will demonstrate how focusing on the multitudes of media in the film offers productive ways of understanding the work in its entirety. Understanding the rich presence, and consequently the important functions, of media leads the way towards a new understanding of this classic.

In Chapter 3, Cinematic Theatre, we will analyse *Birdman* (Alejandro G. Iñárritu 2014), taking as a starting point the role theatre and music play in the film. Our aim is to discuss how the film combines elements of traditional art forms with influences from contemporary media culture (the superhero theme from comics and blockbuster movies, and the cultural influence of YouTube-videos) in order to tell us something about human relations in contemporary society. In this case study, special attention will be paid to how the film was made, and the use of camera, acting, and *mise en scène.* We will also address the extensive use of intermedial references in the film, taken from cinema and literature.

Chapter 4, A Novelist on Film?, investigates the idea of media as bridges and obstacles. We argue that the film, depicting a family traumatised by the death of the mother, investigates the significance of mediation. Photography plays the most prominent part in the film's identity puzzle, but computer games and especially literature also serve as vehicles for meetings between humans struggling with grief. One aim in this chapter is to demonstrate the different roles different media play, on both aesthetic and thematic levels, and we will do this through a close reading as well as discussions on medium specificity.

Chapter 5, Between Cinema and Photography, analyses Jan Troell's *Everlasting Moments* (2008). *Everlasting Moments* deals with existential and psychological questions of memory, time and individual freedom (particularly for women). Our analysis will work through these questions by way of a discussion of specific scenes in the film relating to the temporal form of photography, as mediated by cinema. Troell seems to be searching for a cinematic language somewhere between the flow of cinema and the stillness of photography. The film also provides a miniature historical overview of media in the twentieth century, and the chapter will accordingly also discuss media development over time, from shadow theatre, via analogue photography, to digital cinema.

Unlike the preceding case studies, the sixth study, Mixing Senses and Media, deals with an almost exaggeratedly mixed film – Epstein and Friedman's *Howl* (2010). Here, the mixing of fundamentally different film forms (documentary, biopic and animation), media, and historical epochs, does not need to be teased out, but rather needs systematising and contextualisation in order to be properly understood and, in this case, even criticised.

Chapter 7, Surveilling Media, will demonstrate the possibility of analysing contemporary mainstream productions using the three-step model. An overall description of what we call the intermedial structure of the film will make up the introduction to this chapter, and the thematic and ethical debate related to the issue of torture will be incorporated into a broader discussion of mediation, visibility and surveillance (three questions intimately connected to questions of media and intermediality), by way of the intermedial approach. *Zero Dark Thirty* has been praised for its authentic take on the 'true' story about the hunt for Osama bin Laden, but we will demonstrate the importance of mediation, and particularly of screens (and off-screen) in the film, and discuss the ethical implications of these aesthetic choices.

In Chapter 8, Cinematic Representations of a 'Super Wicked Problem': Climate Change in Documentary Film, we turn to another narrative cinematic form, namely documentary. Our two examples, Luc Jacquet's *Ice and the Sky* (2015), and Jeff Orlowski's *Chasing Ice* (2012), deal with melting polar ice as the ultimate sign of climate change. We do not really doubt the possibilities of visual media to represent climate change for a larger public, but we attempt to view documentary as a cinematic form in the light of intermedial theory and analytical concepts. We hope the discussion will offer a slightly new way of understanding documentary cinema.

In our final chapter, the results of the case studies are summarised, and the proposed analytical model's value to a general cinematic analytical approach is discussed. We here also reflect on possible ways to take our intermedial perspective on film analysis further.

Notes

1. The Kinetoscope was an early motion picture exhibition device invented by Thomas A. Edison which created an illusion of moving images. The Theatreoscope was invented by R. W. Paul to show 35 mm film for the first time.
2. What we will call a qualified medium, see definition below.
3. A useful distinction between interart studies and intermediality is presented by Clüver (2007); (Rajewsky 2014) and Elleström (2010) also offer helpful descriptions of the field.
4. For an overview of the debate within adaptation studies about the difference between cinema and literature, see Elliott (2003). For an example of an analysis actively discussing the medium specificity debate, see Gjelsvik (2013).
5. On the history of the *ut pictura* concept, see Henryk Markiewicz and Uliana Gabara (1987) and concerning Lessing's *Laocoön*, see Sternberg (1999).

6. See also Elliott (2003) about this debate. For a general discussion of medium specificity, see Carroll (1996); for a discussion of the ideas of medium specificity and visual arts, see Mitchell (2005), whereas Chatman (1980) offers a classical discussion of film versus literature from a medium specificity perspective.
7. See John Durham Peters (Peters 1999), who argues against the idealising notion of communication as face-to-face dialogue, and instead demonstrates a long struggle – ranging from Plato to the Internet – between two notions of communication.
8. This article provides a useful summary of different types of references to paintings, and discusses the tabloux vivant more in detail, including Majewksi's work.
9. We are here further developing a method for intermedial analysis of narrative literature suggested by Bruhn (2016a).
10. See the website The Art of the Title, which is dedicated to title sequences, for more on this: http://www.artofthetitle.com/title/sherlock-holmes (last accessed 30 December 2017).

2 Media Behind the Scenes: Orson Welles's *Citizen Kane*

To choose Orson Welles's *Citizen Kane* as our first case study may seem *daring* – can anything new be said about this classic of classics? – but, perhaps, also *conventional* – do all film books necessarily have to discuss *Citizen Kane*? We have chosen *Citizen Kane* because we believe our intermedial analysis can add some productive perspectives to the already rich and rewarding literature surrounding the film. Last but not least, this case study will demonstrate that although our main focus is contemporary cinema, our approach can also be applied to historical films.

Critics hailed *Citizen Kane* as a masterpiece more or less from its first screenings in 1941, although it initially was a financial failure. For instance, it figured at the top of the British film magazine *Sight and Sound*'s famous list of the best films in the world in 1962, 1972, 1982, 1992 and 2002.[1] In spite of the fact that the film's immediate historical context is no longer as obviously urgent (and thus scandalous) as it was for its contemporary spectators, there is no denying that it still has the power to make us reflect upon our current political and mass media climate. The many and relatively unambiguous references to the business and newspaper tycoon William Randolph Hearst (1853–1951) are, for most spectators today, not so easy to detect and not so immediately alarming, but new candidates for allegorical interpretations of Charles Foster Kane in the film are, unfortunately, still close at hand: when Laura Mulvey wrote a new preface to her short monograph on the film in 1992, she stressed that Rupert Murdoch in many ways fitted the Kane figure perfectly, while as we write this Donald Trump has, by applying an efficient but cynical mix of populism and downright lies, risen all the way to the presidency of the United States of America.[2]

Before we move on, a short paraphrasing of the film may be useful. Please note that this summary mainly focuses on the narrative, and does not stress the stylistic or metafictive or intermedial levels of the film that we will later dive into.

In terms of genre, the film may be characterised as a fictional biopic: it pretends to represent the life of a famous man, Charles Foster Kane, from childhood to old age, via his amazing successes and painful failures in business, politics, and love. The film takes place from around 1900 to 1955 in the USA. Instead of establishing a single, homogenising view, the film produces six different perspectives on Kane's life, adding up to a complex psychological and historical portrait. The general perspective is an attempt from reporters to make a newsreel version of his life, which, after a brief, dramatic depiction of Kane's death, introduces the film. The reporters admit the failure of their attempt, and more specifically they believe that if they understand the meaning of his dying word, 'Rosebud', the enigma of the great man will be solved. A reporter is sent to search for better sources on the true meaning and essence of Kane's life, and he interviews five people closely related to Kane.

These perspectives on *Citizen Kane* are presented through five flashbacks that basically constitute the film. The first flashback is provided by Kane's second wife, Susan Alexander Kane, at the El Rancho nightclub; the second his (deceased) guardian, Walter Park Thatcher, whose diary the reporter reads; for the third, the reporter interviews Kane's longtime friend Jedidiah Leland, now living in a nursing home; in a fourth flashback we return to the El Rancho nightclub to the interview with Susan Alexander Kane, and the fifth and last interview is with Kane's butler Raymond, who reveals to the reporter the final, unhappy years of Susan and Charles's life at his luxury castle Xanadu. The reporter does not succeed in solving the enigma, but the spectators see, in some of the final shots of the film, that 'Rosebud' was the name of an old snow sled that Charles played with as a child. The sled is being burned as simple trash after Kane's death.

The historical and political contexts surrounding the film have loomed large in criticism of *Citizen Kane*, in particular in the early critical engagements with it. In addition, the fascinating dramatic twists and turns concerning the writing of the manuscript, and the questions regarding how big a part Herbert Mankiewicz played in the writing process compared to Orson Welles, have been important.[3] Welles's famous contract negotiations with the RKO studio, as well as the production and postproduction of the film, have been subject to some scrutiny, as has the relationship of *Citizen Kane* to some of Welles's earlier or later productions.[4]

It almost goes without saying that the formal and technical achievements of the film have been discussed intensely, particularly with regard to Gregg Toland's indispensable contributions to the cinematographic features and to Bernhard Hermann's musical soundtrack. Apart from being analysed in book-length studies and in specialised articles, these and other formal aspects also play an important role in Bordwell and Thompson's influential neo-formalistic textbook *Film Art. An Introduction* (2017). Here, *Citizen Kane* plays a key role because the film exemplifies almost all of the formal analytical categories developed and described in Bordwell and Thompson's book. Thus, the sophisticated storytelling of *Citizen Kane* occupies a position in film studies (the extremely atypical case study, that nevertheless demonstrates numerous analytical problems) that Marcel Proust's *A la recherche du temps perdu* occupied in Gérard Genette's in some ways comparable narratological *Summa*, 'Discours du récit' in *Figures III* from 1972 (Genette 1980).[5] *Citizen Kane* and *A la recherche du temps perdu* are seemingly inexhaustible treasure chests of narrative *finesse*, in words or in audiovisual form, that exemplify almost any imaginable formal and narratological problem. '*Kane* is an ideal occasion to test how principles of film narrative can work in both familiar and fresh ways', as Bordwell and Thompson remark when introducing a long discussion of the film (Bordwell and Thompson 2017). We will try to demonstrate in this chapter that a conventional 'narratological' approach à la Bordwell and Thompson cannot grasp the medial features, in this case in *Citizen Kane*, that we find particularly interesting.

Several critics have foregrounded that the labyrinthine and complex form of the narration in the film mimics a convoluted and difficult search, and Noël Carroll has even suggested that the reception of *Citizen Kane* can be divided into two interpretations: an 'enigma' interpretation versus a 'Rosebud' interpretation. In both cases the search for the meaning in Kane's life is a complex question, but whereas the 'enigma' interpretation argues that the film represents the theory according to which 'the nature of a person is ultimately a mystery,' and will remain so, the typical 'Rosebud' interpretation of the film would argue that 'Kane's personality is finally explicable by some such notions as those of 'lost childhood' or 'lost innocence' (Carroll 1998: 153).

Regarding this complexity and the overall convolution of the narration, Mulvey quotes Argentinian writer Jorge Luis Borges's famous notion that *Citizen Kane* is a 'labyrinth without a centre' (1992), and also notes that:

> *Citizen Kane* is a film which is built around the pleasures and problems of decipherment not only, explicitly, in the main subject of the film (the journalist's investigation of the Kane enigma), but also in the fact that it builds in a deciphering spectator by means of its visual language and address.
>
> (Mulvey 1992)

In her monograph, Mulvey argues for a reading that combines the politico-historical contextual facts with a rather heavy-handed psychoanalytical interpretation in contradistinction to more solely formalistic readings.

As this unfairly abbreviated review of trends in the *Citizen Kane*-criticism demonstrates, there is no shortage of valuable, critical perspectives on Welles's masterpiece, and *Citizen Kane* serves to demonstrate not only one but several theoretical or methodological persuasions, which has made Peter Wollen remark that '[t]o write about *Citizen Kane* is to write about the cinema' (quoted from Naremore 2004).

In this chapter, we hope to demonstrate that a three-step intermedial analysis may bring to light supplementary ideas to the ones already brought forth in the responses to Welles. In order to achieve this interpretation and discussion, let us initially offer a first-step media registration.

Step one: Cataloguing media in *Citizen Kane*

As mentioned in the introductory chapter, it is more or less impossible to write down, and thus to reproduce, in a chapter or a student's paper, a comprehensive list of the presence of medialities in a feature film. Therefore, the pragmatic choice is often to choose one or several representative fragments of the film, demonstrate the logic of this precise portion and then to 'scale up' the isolated findings to function as a tendency of the entire film. We also, in the same vein, mentioned the problematics of choosing the right 'representative' fragment. In the case of *Citizen Kane*, we have decided not to catalogue media in the most obviously media-saturated parts of the film, such as the newsreel 'News on the March' sequence, or the otherwise very interesting opening of the film. Instead, we will go through a different part, almost directly after the overture consisting of the death scene of Kane, the 'News on the March', and the discussion amongst the newsmen in the editing room. During this discussion the newsreel is criticised by the editor as failing to understand what a man's life is really about: 'All we saw on that screen is that Charles Foster Kane is dead. I know that.' We are going to catalogue medialities in the subsequent ten minutes, not so much because this is a particularly crucial scene in the film, but rather because we wish to demonstrate how the first step can proceed.

In the following we will highlight in bold the many different kinds of present medialities.

In a cut directly from the editing room we get to a very **lifelike representation** of Susan Alexander (Figure 2.1), which turns out to be a **poster**:

Figure 2.1 Susan Alexander Kane's multiple visual presentations: first, via a lifelike poster . . .

With dramatic diegetic thunder, the camera moves upwards from the **poster** to represent the **neon sign** (Figure 2.2) specifying that this is indeed Susan Alexander.

Figure 2.2 . . . and then a specification by way of a neon sign . . .

Moving yet further, the camera travels up again in order to approach the real model for both poster and neon sign, moving through a **glass roof** (Figure 2.3) (that functions like a medial 'window').

Figure 2.3 . . . and finally through yet another 'medial window', the glass roof of the bar.

On the soundtrack, the **diegetic music** from inside the night club is now combined with the thunder outside, and a giant blast of thunder and lightning takes us through the glass roof and down into the room, where the **diegetical jazz music** takes over. The setting of the night club, of which the jazz music is a part, may be worth noting: in the background we see a simple **stage set**, probably a kind of backdrop for a comic western show, a long way from Susan's former opera ambitions that we later learn about. Whereas the **poster**, **neon signs** and **stage set** are related to qualified media, the scene ends with the use of a long distance call on the **telephone** (technical media), where the reporter tells the headquarters of his lack of results.

Characteristically, the deep focus perspective again adds elegantly to the sound milieu of the film: the music moves into the background, leaving room for the **verbal report** on the phone while at the same time allowing for a short conversation with a waiter at the nightclub – conveying, however, the same message: nothing is being said about 'Rosebud'.

A surprising cut from the dark nightclub to a **statue** seen from below, with extradiegetic, somewhat **solemn music**: the camera moves down and reveals the statue to be on top of a **memorial monument** and the name in **sculpted letters** is WALTER PARKS THATCHER. Zooming out, the memorial is part of what turns out to be a **Thatcher Memorial Library** (the information is given by a female librarian or warden), which the reporter is now being let into. This warden talks on a **telephone** and then allows the reporter into another solemn-looking room, where the **diaries** of Thatcher in the form of a **large book** are carried forth, lit from above as if they were a religious item. The reporter looks into the book, and with him we read **the first words** concerning how Thatcher first met Kane as a boy and, in a dissolve, the white page is overlaid with snowflakes while, in **one image, we see the year of their meeting, 1871**, and a boy playing in the snow (actually riding on the snow sled bearing the name Rosebud . . .). Again a **sign** is used to help with the establishment of the scene, when the boy throws a snowball at **a sign of a house** that reads 'Mrs. Kane's Boarding House'.

Step two: structuring medialities in *Citizen Kane*

The media-focused summary above is intended to give an impression of the rich presence of medialities in a ten-minute fragment of *Citizen Kane.* The fragment, in terms of medialities, is not so important for our specific analysis, but it is highly emblematic of the entire film in several ways with regard to how to structure the presence of media in the film.

To begin with, the film obviously 'uses', inside the diegesis, different medialities to varying effect. In this case it is particularly curious how the media represented play important roles in doing the explanatory work related to, among other things, 'establishing shots'. The first meeting with Susan Alexander at the El Rancho is also analysed by Bordwell and Thompson, and it may be illuminating briefly to point to the differences in our approaches (Bordwell and Thompson 2017).

Under the general heading of 'Style in *Citizen Kane*' Bordwell and Thompson demonstrate admirably how the introductory shots using craning and zooms lead to the face-to-face interview with Susan: 'the film techniques create a penetration into the story space, probing the mystery of the central character [Charles Foster Kane].' We argue not that Bordwell and Thompson do not understand the scene correctly, but that their reading exemplifies what could be called a 'media-blind' analytical approach: focused on the basic cinematographic techniques, the presence and function of medialities are neglected. In order to avoid such a media-blind reading, let us first point out the rather banal observation that, despite the fact that *Citizen Kane* has been hailed as a magnificently cinematic-visual endeavour – and this is what is being effectively highlighted in Bordwell and Thompson's analysis – the visual rhetoric is forced to rely on other represented media inside the film, in particular verbal, written language.[6]

Step one's registering of medialities demonstrates the presence of technical media such as telephones, newspapers and pens that abound in the film, alongside qualified media such as journalism (newsreel footage), operatic song, opera stages, and sculptures. We can characterise this as a kind of oversaturated medialities presence in *Citizen Kane*: a multitude of medialities, each standing for different possibilities and limitations. Taken together it is hard to make sense of all these medialities, but one way of understanding this aspect of the film is to recognise its heterogeneous multiplicity as a kind of value in itself, nicely exemplified in this quote by Paul Arthur (who does not, however, apply a medial vocabulary):

> There is such a swell of diffuse sources, styles, and materials in *Citizen Kane* that the idea that it might univocally be dedicated to the demonstration of any single doctrine is ludicrous. What has characterized this film, and made it an enduring object of critical attention, is that it tries to do everything, to satisfy many masters at once: encapsulate a range of film historical trends and formulas; instigate a reform of Hollywood's narrative conventions; reconcile the prerogatives of popular art and high culture; address the 'great man' theory of history in an age of mass media celebrity.
>
> (Arthur quoted in Naremore 2004: 280)

As a first ordering of this media saturation let us consider the 'unfinished collections' of *Citizen Kane*. Kane collects animals, classical artwork and historical objects, and after his death all this is registered in order to be sold off; this is also investigated by the reporter at the end of the film. Kane's collecting, a recurrent theme through the film, has been rather unsystematic, and we get the impression that it is less a sign of a deep passion for assembling complete collections or an urge to collect aesthetically or historically valuable artefacts than it is either an indication of boredom or of a wish to brag about his wealth.

These unfinished collections – sometimes the goods have not even been unpacked from their protective cargo cases – metaphorically echo another important symbol in the film, the jigsaw puzzles. Stretching our definitions somewhat, the jigsaw puzzles can be considered a qualified medium with a (slight) communicative function. One of the pastimes of Kane's second wife, Susan, inside gloomy Xanadu, which is both a museum of Kane's haphazard collections and a living mausoleum, is assembling puzzles. Susan's puzzles symbolise her boredom as well as her loneliness, but they are also a meta symbol of the hunt for wholeness and ultimately a search for truth and meaning. The puzzles work as a clear parallel to Charles Foster Kane's entire life (so difficult for the journalists to 'assemble'), and so they are, we argue, invested with symbolic value as examples of games or collections that cannot be consummated in satisfactory ways. In one of the film's final scenes we get an overview shot of all the collected goods, which gives an impression of disorder, or even chaos. These are not the objects of a conscientious collector who has taken care of his valuable findings; on the contrary, it is a disorganised compilation of disparate objects. Or, to pursue our suggestion, the unfinished collections are like pieces of jigsaw puzzles that can never be fully assembled. This, we argue, is one medial structure in the film: numerous, scattered medialities as unassembled jigsaw puzzle pieces.

Second, it is possible to construct a comprehensive medial structure in the film that is at least as important as the 'media as jigsaw pieces'. This structure has less to do with the mere presence of medialities in the film, but relates instead to the general way that all media are represented in the film by showing what is going on 'behind the scenes', resulting in a making strange of the medialities that the spectators of the film perhaps thought they understood.[7]

2.1 The trailer for *Citizen Kane*

The spectators exposed to Orson Welles's original trailer, probably in proximity to the news reel section when going to the cinema, would to a certain extent be prepared for the 'behind the scenes' perspective of *Citizen Kane*. In the trailer, Welles shrewdly manages to advertise the coming film while also debunking it in the very same move: This is the case when Orson Welles's 'Godlike, disembodied' (Salmon 2006, and at that point nationally renowned) voice-over asserts that, 'what follows is supposed to advertise our first motion picture. *Citizen Kane* is the title, and we hope it can correctly be called a coming attraction. It is certainly coming, coming to this theatre, and I think our Mercury actors are making it an attraction.' Paul Salmon sees the trailer as an example of Welles being in-between the demands of the commercial market on one hand, and his artistic ambitions on the other: the trailer sheds 'an interesting light on Welles's artistic bind at the time, as he courted a wide, popular audience on the very eve of springing on a largely unsuspecting public the most technically and formally advanced film in Hollywood' (Salmon 2006).

This structure becomes apparent right after the newsreel has been presented in the screening room early in the film. As spectators we eavesdrop on a conversation that we are normally deprived of: the discussions among the editors and reporters about the newsreel is a clear example of the tendency to go 'behind the scenes'. The media product that we have just seen is discussed and criticised and we learn about some of the basics of form and content of this qualified medium called the newsreel.[8] Later on, when Kane enters the newspaper business, we witness an example of the same structure: we hear more about the production and hiring and economic considerations than about what is actually being written in the newspaper. We understand what a newspaper is from 'behind the scenes'.

And a third, grand example of this 'behind the scenes' process is Kane's attempt to make his wife Susan into an opera star. Welles gives us this story in two parts: first (recounted in the Jedidiah Leland flashback section), where we jump almost immediately to the terrible failure at her debut performance, which is preceded by a spectacular craning scene. After seeing the hectic preparations just before the theatre curtain rises, the camera moves with the curtain upwards, through the nooks and crannies of the lines controlling the theatre machinery, ending up on top of the theatre, where two workers stand looking down on the stage. Tellingly, one of them silently pinches his nose, signalling 'this performance stinks.' This brief but powerful example of getting 'behind the scenes' (or above the stage) is, however, followed shortly after in the next flashback section when Susan herself narrates her training as an opera singer (an impossible project, because she cannot sing!). In her own words, and at a slower tempo, she brings us to the identical failure on stage. The 'behind the scenes' representations here are focused more on her unsuccessful training, but also on Kane himself revealing that no matter how she sings, the reviews will be good for the very simple reason that he owns the newspapers. The objectivity – or lack of it – of the institution of theatre criticism, too, is revealed in this behind-the-scenes strategy.

On top of the behind-the-scenes debunking of the newsreel, the newspaper, opera and the supposedly free, objective theatre critic, we might add a final 'medium' in a broad sense of the word, namely Kane's castle. Kane's Xanadu, which is the most expensive and luxurious building on Earth (according to the newsreel speaker), is definitely a fictional version of Hearst's 'Hearst Castle' located in San Simeo on the one hand, and of course referring to romantic poet Samuel Taylor

Coleridge's programmatic poetic vision of the same name in the poem 'Kubla Khan', or Kubla Kane?, from 1816 on the other. Xanadu is also a kind of artwork or medium, comprised of the collections mentioned above, yet even Xanadu is, in the end, debunked as an illusion: after the death of Kane we get behind the scenes of the grand house, where its collections and all the magic and luxury are torn away, and it is revealed as just a kind of huge storage facility.

What we argue here is that what looks like ordinary film narration, with psychological and existential effects, of course, can actually be 'translated' into a systematicity that directly relates to the question of represented and internally interacting medialities.

Step three: Contextualising medialities in *Citizen Kane*

In step two we established the existence of two medial strategies: a perspectival jigsaw puzzle idea on the one hand, and a 'behind the scenes', debunking idea on the other. Both make sense inside the diegesis of the film and they both offer valuable ways of organising the presence of media in *Citizen Kane.* One question is how to frame these two structures outside the diegetic world and strategies of the film itself, which is the function of the third step in our model. Another question is: how do these two strategies relate to each other?

Let us, as preparation for answering these questions, go through a few of the important media-related interpretations of *Citizen Kane.* After that we will be able to suggest our own framing perspective on the presence and function of medialities in the film.

In 1981, Lawrence J. Clipper argued that *Citizen Kane* erects a dichotomy between nature – or rather 'reality' – and a broad spectrum of artificial arts: 'This theme of the subjugation of Nature, of Nature being violated for the purposes of art and artifice [. . .] turns out to be a central strand of the narrative materials of *Citizen Kane*' (Clipper 1981). With 'arts and artifice,' Clipper hints at what we above (in step one) characterised as the very rich presence of media. Clipper argues that the main theme of the film is the damaging, estranging influence of arts and artifices over a non-mediated world (to use our own terms), essentially a rather romantically conceived critique, which is not really where we want to take our analysis. Welles, we think, does not reproduce such a clear-cut dichotomy; reality necessarily comes to us via media, *Citizen Kane* shows, but Clipper nevertheless is on the right track of finding a basic dual tendency in the film, even if we don't follow him all the way.

Tony Jackson's 2008 article 'Writing, Orality, Cinema: The "Story" of *Citizen Kane*' offers another useful interpretation, touching even more directly on the questions we are interested in. Jackson provides a systematic interpretation of *Citizen Kane* focused on the question of one specific group of communicative tools (what we call medialities). Jackson pursues the astoundingly rich presence and important function of represented language, written or verbal, in the film. From the capital K in wrought iron on the gates of Xanadu in the opening scene, all the way through the newspaper discussions and the public speeches, and on to the final revelation of the enigma or puzzle of the word 'Rosebud'; the enigma of Rosebud that is revealed in the end of the film, when the old snow sled is burned as simple trash after Kane's death, where this sled is unequivocally identified, by written, painted letters on the wood. Jackson, more than Clipper, leads the way towards the double framing that we want to suggest below. Jackson manages to pursue language in all its different forms in the film and ends up demonstrating how Welles is actually orchestrating what we call a paragone: a competition between the arts, in this case between writing (literature) and moving images (cinema).

Jackson observes that the 'News on the March' newsreel exhibits an almost encyclopaedic mixture of the technological means of telling a man's story at this time in history: the newsreel sequence exhibits picture magazines, photography, painting, newspapers, radio news, and film.[9] We want to broaden what Jackson isolates to the newsreel's medial mixedness to be of importance to the entire film, as we saw in the first step of our analysis. But now we can rephrase this in contextual terms. Media is everywhere in the twentieth century reality, something the film, representing the presence and function of media in everyday and political life, depicts highly accurately. This is the first framing point: *Citizen Kane* offers – in terms of medialities – a realistic depiction of an American historical reality in the first half of the twentieth century.

A second, more abstract point, is to try and investigate Welles's typical way of depicting all these medialities in the double medial gesture we established in step two. While *Citizen Kane* demonstrates the overwhelmingly heterogeneous presence of media (what we called the 'jigsaw puzzle'), the film also constantly, and rather methodically, discloses the function and nature of media by the persistent disclosure from 'behind the scenes' that we pointed to as the second medial mechanism inherent in the film.

The jigsaw metaphor demonstrates that we are defined by media, that 'media determine our situation' as Friedrich Kittler is known for stating (see also our final reflections on Trier's *Louder Than Bombs* in Chapter 4): not necessarily as a negative condition, as Clipper implies in his reading, but neither solely as a positive possibility. And without following the notion further, it seems plausible that Welles's project is inspired by and thus parallel to some of the central tenets of the literary modernism of great writers such as Proust, Woolf, Conrad or Joyce, who all worked actively in their novels to demolish a simplified notion of the existence of one, objective, spatio-temporal reality.

Yet there is another, probably more optimistic idea of the presence of medialities, and the role of these media – both understood as mass media and as communicative tools today, and this is the 'behind the scenes' strategy. The disclosures of this strategy are more activistic; *see*, the film says, *what may occur to us, as spectators and readers sitting at the receiving end of the media chain, is utterly mundane and ideologically fraught but it is nevertheless changeable.* Thus, *Citizen Kane* is as relevant for a modern audience as it was in 1941.

So, we end up with two interesting framings of the presence and function of medialities; that is, two ways of understanding the presence and function of media outside the film. First, media as condition, second, media as what can be criticised, made strange, and consequently changed. To a certain extent we end up in a framing, general interpretation of the film that poses a mediaphobic position (we are conditioned by media) and a more mediaphile position (media are simply social constructions, that can be seen through, and that can be disclosed and changed into something else). Are we, to put it even more directly, slaves of the media and communicative devices – or can we manage to see them as media, *make them strange*, and change them? These are the two models of medialities we find by analysing the medial economy of *Citizen Kane* by way of the three-step analysis.

Conclusion

The dichotomy we ended up with in the last instance of step three is probably a false one; actually, the two models complement rather than exclude one another. Our intermedial interpretation of *Citizen Kane* demonstrates that what is often described as the ubiquity of media in contemporary developed societies was already felt as a condition and consequently represented in Orson Welles's film from 1941; this is the jigsaw puzzle understanding of all the medialities surrounding us, with the risk of feeling lost among them. But even if this is represented as a fact in the film, it seems as if there is also an inherent media optimism in it, meaning that it is indeed possible to get 'behind the scenes' and better understand the nature and functioning of the media. It could be argued that Orson Welles's *Citizen Kane* offers a diagnosis of modern Western mediacentric societies, but also suggests a cure for the impending illnesses of such a media-saturated society: namely, to represent such societies aesthetically, on film in this case, with all the medial complexities and contradictions that this produces, in order to better understand and see through these medial presences.

Welles produced this statement decades ago, in an epoch that seen from our mediated society might look easy to understand and rather underdeveloped, media-wise, compared to what we experience today. But instead of focusing on the differences, perhaps we should try to better understand the similarities? We are still surrounded by media, they influence our love life and our politics and everything in between, and the medialities seem to function more and more like prosthetic, technical limbs to our bodies. The question is whether we still believe that we ever get a privileged perspective behind the scenes of our media prostheses? Is this even possible any longer? Despite the fact that *Citizen Kane* in many ways is a pessimistic film that depicts the unhappiness of human life and the corruption of politics, it also does seem to be more optimistic, or simply naïve, regarding the possibilities of actually accessing a 'behind the scenes' perspective on our media and their roles in modern life.

Perhaps less controversially, we have tried to demonstrate, by way of the intermedial analysis, that *Citizen Kane* is certainly, as critics have stressed repeatedly in their responses, a film about perspectivism and the difficulties of reaching a truth about any man or woman's life, or about the world in general. *Citizen Kane* is indeed a 'celluloid rebus' (Laura Mulvey 1992: 33). We have argued that this classical position in the rich seam of *Citizen Kane* criticism can be argued for in intermedial terms instead of in terms of thematics, psychoanalytical theory or narratological analysis. Understanding the presence and function of medialities offers another version of the same insight, but also adds some important and new nuances to it.

Notes

1. In 2012 it was overthrown by Alfred Hitchcock's *Vertigo* (1958). See more about the lists http://www.bfi.org.uk/news/50-greatest-films-all-time (last accessed 30 December 2017). For a general overview of the early reception of *Citizen Kane* see Naremore (2004).
2. As it happens, *Citizen Kane* is Donald Trump's favourite movie! Filmmaker Errol Morris interviewed Trump regarding his understanding of *Citizen Kane* (Audi 2016).
3. The famous film critic Pauline Kael wrote the controversial essay 'Raising Kane' in 1971 where she discredited Welles and foregrounded Mankiewicz's contributions to the script. Her essay, however, has since been heavily criticised by film scholars and other critics.
4. A specific discussion of the making of the film is dealt with in Carringer (1996) and a range of critical responses to *Citizen Kane* is found in Gottesman (1971) Finally, Welles's biographical background received a detailed representation in McGilligan (2015).
5. Translated as *Narrative Discourse. An Essay in Method* in 1980.
6. The film's constant reliance on verbal language has been pointed out by Jackson (2008), to which we will return below.
7. The 'making strange' here refers more to the Russian Formalist idea that art has the potential to make us perceive the world anew, if it offers new ways of representing it; in Bertolt Brecht's subsequent notion of 'Verfremdung' this aesthetic function is invested with ideological (Marxist) notions, which is probably not the most important feature in *Citizen Kane.*

8. Between 1910 and 1960 it was common to show a newsreel before the feature film in cinemas around the world. These newsreels were a compilation of short documentaries that would provide the audience with the latest news, a service that was eventually taken over by television news.
9. Jackson's inspiring article also offers a comparison between the literary style of Joseph Conrad and the style and medial affordances of *Citizen Kane* and cinema:

> But on a broader level, the juxtaposition of Welles and Conrad can serve to dissolve the disciplinary boundaries between literature and film studies, revealing how the characteristics of both media came to be defined in relation to each other in the modernist period. For Welles takes from Conrad's works not only the structuring use of frame narratives and multiple perspectives, but also Conrad's concern with the relationship among speech, writing, and image, a relationship being transformed in the late nineteenth and early twentieth century by Welles's own new medium of cinema and new technologies of sound recording.
>
> (Jackson 2008)

3 Cinematic Theatre: Alejandro G. Iñárritu's *Birdman*

> The cinema and the theatre exist in a dialectical tension. Put an actor onstage, it's theatre; record the performance with a movie camera, it's cinema. Film a person at the counter of a drugstore, it's cinema; take the camera away, it's not theatre; add a spectator and it is.
>
> (Brody 2014)

It is neither controversial, nor original, to claim that *Birdman* is a film about theatre. This is simply stating the obvious: the film is about a former film star, Riggan (played by Michael Keaton), who, in order to reclaim his status and self-esteem, decides to direct and act in a Broadway play, that he himself has also adapted for the stage.

When it comes to the recurring questions regarding cinema and medium specificity, comparisons between theatre and film have had a prominent position historically as well as in contemporary discussions (see the Introduction). Many theorists have taken turns discussing how cinema differs from theatre and vice versa. Philosopher Stanley Cavell, who has theorised the ontology of cinema, pins the difference between the two media on their different relationship with the actor: 'The obvious difference is that in theater we are in the presence of an actor, in a movie house we are not', and he goes on to pinpoint the difference by writing that 'in a play the character is present, whereas in a film the actor is' (Cavell 1992). We will take the opportunity to discuss the actor in this chapter, one of the major elements in cinema that are often overlooked in film studies. Our aim is twofold; we want to illuminate differences between the two media, both on an ontological level (related to medium specificity), and on a contextual level (related to the two media's statuses in contemporary culture).

Stanley Cavell's discussion of this topic, as is the case with many others who have written about film and theatre, is inspired by the classical film theorist André Bazin, as are we (Hanssen 2013a, b). Few theorists have been as important as André Bazin when it comes to discussing and defining cinema, and his perspectives on film and theatre can illuminate the complex relationship between media in Alejandro G. Iñárritu's acclaimed film. The difference between theatre and cinema can be captured in the medium's relation to space, according to Bazin.

The theatre scene can be understood as a physically enclosed space, 'by virtue of the fact that nothing lies beyond it, the way painting exists by virtue of its frame' (Bazin 2009b). The film image, on the contrary, always refers to a space outside itself, according to Bazin (Frisvold Hanssen 2013b: 54). Bazin also provides general perspectives related to our over-all questions in this book, and his theoretical framework can even be said to be rooted in an 'intermedial point of view' (Frisvold Hanssen 2013b). Summing up Bazin's work in this respect, Frisvold Hanssen claims: 'Bazin's film theory is in many respects an account of various processes of transfer where the physical and material existence and qualities of film images have repercussions for how we understand and interact with what is being 'multiplied' by the film medium' (ibid). In the following we will investigate some of the relations between theatre and cinema in *Birdman*.

Birdman is a film in which the comparison between cinema and theatre is at the core of its form and topic; while some critics have called it a film about film, or 'what cinema can do or be' (Collin 2015), others have claimed it to be 'the best film about theatre ever made' (Trueman 2015). When describing theatre, Bazin foregrounds the importance of presence, relating this to the role actors, time and space play, a relationship we also will foreground in our discussion of *Birdman*, or to give it its full title, *Birdman or (The Unexpected Virtue of Ignorance)*. Special attention will be given to the elements that Bazin and Cavell foregrounded: the staging of space and the presence of the actor. In particular, we will draw attention to the way the camerawork in the film is used to create illusions of time and space, and to portray the actors on-stage and off-stage, thus framing and illuminating differences and similarities between film and theatre, but in this chapter we want to go one step further and discuss the film as 'cinematic theatre'. However, while theatre and the physical stage is important in the film, and is most important in our discussion here, we will also draw attention to other medialities in the film, from blockbuster movies and social media via literature, jazz and classical music. Media play different roles in this film, and in *Birdman* intertextual and heteromedial references play a major part.

Synopsis and reception

Birdman tells the story of Riggan Thomson, a Hollywood star whose career has been in decline since he left the blockbuster superhero franchise *Birdman* two decades previously. In an attempt to halt his career's descent from celebrity to 'has-been', he adapts a Raymond Carver short story (*What We Talk About When We Talk About Love*) for the St James Theatre on Broadway, where he directs the theatre adaptation, with himself in a major role.[1] When the film begins, the show is in big trouble: one of the actors is a terrible actor, but he soon has a mysterious accident (probably caused by Riggan, who is able to practice telekinesis), and the producer Jake (Zack Galifinakis) is worried about both finances and publicity. Broadway star Mike Shiner (!) (Edward Norton) is hired as a replacement, which adds to the conflicts at the theatre. Riggan's daughter, Sam (Emma Stone), who is just out of rehab for her drug addiction, has been hired as his assistant, his ex-wife Sylvia (Amy Ryan) is worried that Riggan is not looking after their daughter, and his lover and fellow actress Laura (Andrea Riseborough) thinks she is pregnant with his child. And Mike ends up having an affair with Sam. Thus, the basic storyline clearly echoes the theme of the Carver plot they are performing, which again echoes Riggan's own life, both in relation to his own unfaithfulness and his depression, with also possibly a tendency toward alcoholism.

During a preview of the play Riggan accidentally gets locked out of the theatre and photos and videos of the incident go viral via social media. Riggan also gets drunk and insults Broadway's most powerful theatre critic, of the *New York Times*, who threatens to 'kill' his play. On the day of the opening Riggan wakes up hungover in the street, with the recurring voice of the superhero Birdman in his head, then Birdman turns up in person for the first time in the film in a sequence that resembles scenes from a blockbuster movie, complete with soldiers, helicopters and monsters on Broadway. On the night the play opens, Riggan swaps the prop gun with a real gun and then shoots himself live on stage in the play's finale, to a standing ovation from an audience unaware that they have witnessed a real suicide attempt. Riggan survives, and wakes up in hospital with an injured nose, a rave review from the *New York Times* reviewer, who celebrates his performance as being super-realistic, and praises the play for shedding (much needed) real blood on stage.

Birdman received nine Oscar nominations in 2015, and won four major awards.[2] The film could be said to be Mexican director Alejandro G. Iñárritu's major breakthrough in Hollywood, and it is still the best-received film of his career. His first Mexican film *Amores Perros* (2000) was a huge success, after which his Hollywood career developed with *Babel* (2012), which won him an Oscar, as did his next film *The Revenant* (2015). The critical reception of *Birdman* was overwhelmingly positive: in addition to acclaim for the acting, directing, screenplay and cinematography, a striking tendency in the reviews is the way critics compare the movie with other films and artworks. The list of references in the reviews includes films such as Hitchcock's *The Rope*, John Cassavettes's *The Opening Night*, Wim Wender's *Wings of Desire*, several of Godard's films, as well as Cervantes's Renaissance novel *Don Quixote*, and the Greek myth depicting the rise and fall of Icarus (Dargis 2014, Brody 2014, Bradshaw 2014, Collin 2015). This last reference is found in Manohla Dargis's review in *New York Times*. While Dargis was originally worried about the result of Iñárritu's maximalism meeting Carver's minimalism, she ends up praising what she describes as the film's enjoyable excess, flawless acting and astonishing camerawork:

> Iñárritu [. . .] has staged and shot the movie so that it looks like everything that happens, from airborne beginning to end, occurs during one transporting continuous take. The camera doesn't just move with the story and characters, it also ebbs and flows like water, soars and swoops like a bird, its movement as fluid as a natural element, as animated as a living organism.
>
> (Dargis 2014)

The *Guardian*'s Peter Bradshaw claimed that the film made him feel that he could fly, and he was almost tricked into believing that the film was shot more or less in one take, which of course is the feeling Luzbeki and Iñárritu have tried to achieve by way of the long-take aesthetics dominating the film (Bradshaw 2014). In a more negative review, Richard Brody of the *New Yorker* discusses the long take as one of the major tropes in modernist cinema, but states that, 'In 'Birdman,' the long take converts cinema to theatre – and back' (Brody 2015). Later, we will discuss the camerawork and the repeated use of long takes in the film.

Although some critics found the film to be a little too much and rather empty, most celebrated its craftsmanship. Robbie Collin in the *Telegraph* expressed a reoccurring critical perspective on the film:

> Birdman isn't a piece of empty showmanship. It's a piece about empty showmanship [. . .]. This is grand, spectacular, star-powered cinema – a cosmological blockbuster – that makes us ask again what cinema can do and be.
>
> (Collin 2015)

In the following we will discuss the relationship between cinema and theatre, in particular the question about *presence*, and we will start with by cataloguing and discussing the presence of other art forms and medialities in *Birdman.*

Step one: cataloguing media in *Birdman*

As mentioned already we consider the film to be 'about' the relationship between cinema and theatre, cinematic theatre, and the following cataloguing of medialities in two sequences in the film will demonstrate how different aspects of theatre and cinema are foregrounded and, in particular, how they enter into interesting relationships with each other. Since the film is so rich in intertexual and heteromedial references pointing towards a long list of art forms, we will only present a catalogue of medialities in two illustrative sequences: the opening of the film (where the film star turns actor/director on Broadway), and the incident where Riggan is locked out of the theatre (where the actor becomes a new kind of star). We mark the presence of medialities in **bold**.

The film opens with the **sound of drums**, and the **names** of the **production companies** involved, followed by **red letters** on a **black**

background, in alphabetical order.[3] The letters appear as if written by **a typewriter** before our eyes, following the **rhythm of the drums**, until they read:

> And did you get what you wanted from this life, even so?
> I did.
> And what did you want?
> To call myself beloved, to feel myself beloved on the earth.
>
> (Raymond Carver, *Late Fragment*)[4]

And then, the title *Birdman (The Unexpected virtue of Ignorance)* in **white letters**. Next we see a short **clip** of a meteor burning up, and then we are introduced to Riggan, sitting (or rather, levitating in the air) in his underwear with his back towards us in his wardrobe at **St James Theatre**. We hear a **hoarse voice** that after a while we realise is the voice of **Birdman** telling Riggan that they should not be in this horrible place.

Riggan's meditation is interrupted by the sound of an incoming **Skype call**, and he moves over to his **computer** where he receives a **video call** from his daughter. When he closes the laptop, the **poster** of Riggan as Birdman on the wall is reflected together with Riggan's tired face in the **mirror**. He is called on **stage** and the camera follows him in a **long uninterrupted take** as he walks down the theatre's stairs and corridors, passing different workers on his way, before entering the stage, where he starts to interact with the three **actors** rehearsing his own **adaptation** of the Carver **short story** *What We Talk About When We Talk About Love.* As he enters he is met by his **theatre producer**, and Riggan tells the producer that he would feel better if Ray could start **acting**. Here the sound changes from focusing on the **drums**, to **dialogue**. The camera continues to move, but now in circles on the **stage** where a scene in a kitchen is taking place, closing in on the **actors**' faces as they deliver their **lines**. Riggan leaves **character** to instruct the **actor**, but can't hide his irritation. After Riggan stares at a lamp over them, it falls down and injures the actor, Riggan and **camera** move away from the commotion and back to his wardrobe. The **voice of Birdman** blurs into the **sound of the drums**. The producer follows Riggan and they discuss possible replacements for the actor: Riggan asks for **Woody Harrelson** and the producer answers: 'He is doing the next ***Hunger Games***'. When he suggests **Michael Fassbender**, the answer is that he is doing the prequel for the ***X-Men*** prequel. **Jeremy Renner** 'He was nominated', 'The ***Hurt Locker*** guy' . . . 'He is an **Avenger**'. As they enter the wardrobe **Robert Downey Jr** is on the **television** being interviewed about ***The Avengers***. Riggan sits down in front of his **mirror** and with the image of Birdman; the voice is back, criticising what he calls Downey's tin man (**Iron Man**) as a poor **image of a superhero**.

Riggan smashes the pot with flowers that had been placed there and we get the first visible cut, to a scene in the wardrobe where Riggan is being **interviewed** by some journalists about his move to theatre: 'Why would anyone go from playing the lead in a **comic book franchise** to adapting **Carver for** the **stage**?', asks one of them, and he goes on to quote the French philosopher **Roland Barthes**. A female journalist interrupts Riggan's answer: 'OK, hang on, who is this Barthes guy? Which *Birdman* was he in?' Her next question is about some gossip she found on **Twitter**, and a Chinese journalist who doesn't speak English very well gets excited when he thinks that he hears that Riggan will play in ***Birdman 4***. The producer comes back and throws the journalists out, he is worried about a feature story in' **'the *Times*'**, while Riggan takes away the **Birdman poster**. Lesley knocks on the door and tells them that Mike Shiner is available for the part, which makes the producer excited because theatre critics 'love him'. Jake walks down the stairs, asks the technician to put on the lights and here, seconds later, Mike (Edward Norton) appears on stage, talking about all the actors who have played on the same stage before them: **Marlon Brando, Jason Robards, Helen Hayes**. Mike and Riggan start to play out the scene, rehearsing the lines, while the camera moves around as previously, but this time it is Mike who takes over the role of director and comes back with suggestions to simplify and thus improve Riggan's **manuscript**. The scene ends with Sam coming to bring Mike to do **costumes**, and as they walk away she tells him how good she thinks he has been in the **theatre productions** she has seen him play in.

The next scene we want to address is a carefully crafted scene, moving back and forth between the **performance** of **the play** and life behind the curtains. Mike and Sam play a **game** of 'truth and dare', where Mike always picks truth, whereas Sam urges him to choose dare. During their conversation, he says that he always pretends, except when he is **on stage**. We follow Sam and Mike into the loft of the theatre, where they have sex. Then the camera changes perspective, to the action taking place on the stage below them, and then moves down from the ceiling (or rather, it floats like a feather) getting closer and closer to Riggan. When it lands on stage it moves towards Riggan, who performs his monologue in front of the audience.

As he utters Carver's line 'So, I guess the question we should ask ourselves is, "what do we talk about when we talk about love?"' the camera has moved up close, and we see Riggan's face in **close-up** profile. At that moment, the **stage lights** are turned off, the room gets dark and the audience applaud.

Riggan leaves the front of the stage, and while changing costume and fixing his make-up he and Laura talk about what it would be like if she in fact had been pregnant; the conclusion being that they would raise a kid like **Justin Bieber** (the way she says it indicates that this reference to the celebrity wonder kid is to be understood as a negative thing). While she returns to the **stage** (where she delivers **lines** about her unwanted child), Riggan catches a glimpse of Mike and Sam kissing backstage. In a new close-up, we watch Riggan's face change, from the excitement of performing live in front of an audience to a feeling of distress entering from the world outside. He decides to have a smoke in the open air, but gets locked out. The world outside turns out to be a mixture of **autograph hunters**, **a brass band** performing, the large **neon signs** on Times Square, tourists, a guy in a **Spiderman costume**, several bystanders following Riggan with **cameras** and **cell phones**,[5] and a **cacophony of sounds**: **drums**, traffic, men and women shouting, laughter. On his way back through the main entrance several of the employees try to stop him, but he walks down the aisle towards the stage at the exact timing of the line 'What are you doing here?' Back in wardrobe, Sam shares the **news** of him becoming a trending topic in the **virtual sphere**, with 350,000 viewers in less than an hour: 'Believe it or not, this is power'.

As this detailed description of the two sequences demonstrates, the film is overwhelmingly full of references to media forms, including technical media, but in particular blockbuster films and theatre, and also actors and authors.

Step two: structuring medialities in *Birdman*

To begin with, and on a general level, let us simply ascertain that *Birdman*, primarily because of its subject matter, visualises a lot of the work that goes on behind the scenes in a theatre. We get a lively impression of the hectic activities involving the producer, light technician, make-up artists, and more. It becomes clear that what may seem, for the theatre spectator, to be a glimpse of real life through the so-called fourth wall of realist theatre is, indeed, a staged and crafted artistic vision. This, of course, is comparable to one of the main media structures we established in the previous chapter, on *Citizen Kane*, the 'behind-the-scenes' structure. In addition, music plays an important role (Antonio Sánchez's percussive jazz score in combination with a range of classical music, including Mahler, Tchaikovsky, Rachmaninov and Ravel), while several other media occupy minor roles (such as posters, games, social media and YouTube).

Literature is a particularly interesting case in point. Raymond Carver's short story is the source for the play inside the film, and since Carver's original text is to a large degree based on dialogue, several of the lines are used directly, as they were written by Carver. When Mike encourages Riggan to make the dialogue simpler, he is in fact arguing that Carver's prose should be minimised. This is in itself an interesting take, since Carver has often been described as a literary minimalist.[6] However, *What We Talk About When We Talk About Love* (as well as the collection with the same name) has also become a prominent example of the relationship between a writer and his editor, since the published version was much shorter than Carver's original manuscript, due to heavy editing by his editor Gordon Lish.[7] If we were to stretch the interpretation of the different roles here, we could argue that Mike could be seen as impersonating Lish, with Riggan being closer to Carver. Carver's short story could be said to function as a meta-commentary on Riggan's biography, since several of the elements here are of relevance to his life, such as the role of love and his problems relating to alcohol and mental illness, as well as the ways that the short story echoed Carver's own life.

The film's use of both these medialities (theatre and literature) foregrounds the role of the creation of art, and of how works of art are the outcome of collaboration between different people. Thus, *Birdman* can be described as meta-cinema. Such types of film often focus on or follow a film production (see, for instance, Godard's *Le Mepris* (1963), Fellini's *8½* (1963) or Michael Winterbottom's *A Cock and Bull Story* (2005)), but we argue that here, although we follow a theatre production, *Birdman* also comments on film as an art form.[8] It does this, for example, in the way its form underlines specific cinematic elements. Two major cinematic techniques are important in the film as a whole, and particularly so in the two sequences we are scrutinising here: the *long take*, and the *close-up*.

3.1 The long take

Cinematographer Emmanuel Lubezki is famous for his spectacular long takes; before *Birdman*, his work could be seen in Alfonso Cuarón's *Children of Men* (2006), a director for whom the long take is a recurring motif.[9] This aesthetic approach could be seen as an opposition to a more montage-driven form, which is more of a norm in classical Hollywood cinema (see, for example Bordwell, Staiger, and Thompson (1985), Isaacs (2016)). A long take can be described as a 'sequence shot of excessive duration' (Isaacs 2016), and in *Birdman* most of the long takes vary from 7–15 minutes, which are unusually extended long takes.[10] In addition to reflecting different periods and different auteurs' approach to film style, the long take can also illuminate the role of film technology.[11] The development of different cameras – the Steadicam, for example – in the mid-1970s, and the later change from analogue to digital filmmaking, have influenced the use of long takes. Famously, Alfred Hitchcock wanted *Rope* (1984) to give the illusion of being shot in one take, but the cameras of the time could only hold enough 35 mm film for 10 minutes. In *Birdman*, both Steadicam and hand-held cameras are used. As formulated by Isaacs: 'the sequence shot [a long take that constitutes a whole sequence] as a spatial and temporal designation is only appropriate, in its purest sense, to filmic technology' (Isaacs 2016). In *Birdman*, the digital camera is used to create a unique experience of time and space, where we are intended to feel that we are following the characters through St James Theatre (and on to Times Square) as events take place, although the film's diegesis covers a few days, not two hours. A likely inspiration for the specific use of long takes used in *Birdman* is Michael Ballhaus's famous shot in Martin Scorsese's *Goodfellas* (1990).

The second prominent cinematic device used to great effect in *Birdman* is the close-up. Throughout the history of film theory, scholars, as well as directors, have differed on what they have regarded as the preferred cinematic techniques (montage, *mise en scène*, long take, close-up, and so on). Bazin's position, for instance, was that the long take should be used when it could strengthen the realism in a film, and that a moving long take – a technique used to extremes in *Birdman* – would draw attention to the camera, as indeed it does in this film (Bazin 2009b). The camera in *Birdman* constantly moves up and down stairs, or circles around the actors on the stage, in ways that also emphasise how cinema might differ from a theatre experience, where we are usually restricted to the perspective from our own seat in the theatre. For the film spectator, this means being able to see something up close.

The close-up has had a special position in film theory, most notably in the writings of Béla Balázs, Jean Epstein and, to some extent, Gilles Deleuze. For the classical film theorist Béla Balázs, the close-up in cinema was essential in order to capture intimacy and the 'soul of man', because we can follow the movements in a person's face over time (Balázs 1924). The aim for the cinematic medium, accordingly, should be to develop into an independent art by using a different language form than theatre (Balázs 1924; Andrew 1976). This would occur, for example, through the change of perspective and angles, as well as by breaking up the scenes by way of montages. In *Birdman*, the close-up is used particularly when Riggan is on stage, both during rehearsals and when he is performing in front of a live audience. So, we are not only moving around with him, we are also able to look at him in close-up, getting behind his performance, so to speak, making visible not only the actor but the person behind the mask. Overall the long take in combination with close-ups could be said to add to the feeling of being present at this given time and place: 'The long take and emphatic presence of the hand-held apparatus intensifies the materiality of place, time, and a spectatorial subjectivity within the pro-filmic environment' (Isaacs 2016:11). In the case of *Birdman*, the most important pro-filmic elements (the elements in front of the camera) are the *mise en scène* of the St James Theatre and the actors, who are used to create the feeling of being at the theatre. To put it another way, both these cinematic techniques are used to explore the illusion of the theatre, which brings us back to our initial hypothesis – that *Birdman* seems to address the difference between theatre and cinema, or between art and mass culture. This is a long, complicated and ongoing debate that we will move on to discuss more in detail in the final step of our analysis.

In the second step of this case study analysis, we have focused not only on theatre and literature but on two cinematic devices, the long take and the close up: these may not appear to be specifically *intermedial* structures rather than internally cinematic devices. Let us at this point simply sum up our findings, by reminding the reader that Iñárritu and Lubezki go to great lengths to hide the cuts (as well as to cover the time jumps through means other than montage), by turning off the lights when Riggan receives applause on stage to disguise the cut between his monologue and his exit, or by having people passing corners or mirrors where the cut is concealed. In the same way, the close-ups, eminently cinematic devices as they are, actually also work in the direction of making the spectators feel that they are present, in the theatre.

Step three: framing the structured medialities in *Birdman*

From an intermedial point of view *Birdman* illuminates what theatre is, as well as what cinema is, and we will argue that the film debates the status of the relationship between the two art forms. All the way through the film, and in the scenes we have looked into in particular, there is a tension between high culture (represented by theatre, literature and jazz) and popular culture, represented by superhero movies, social media and celebrity culture. In other words, the film could be said to deliberate or wrangle over which of the two art forms is better. As such it enters the very long tradition of paragone, the competition between the arts that dates back to the Renaissance. It also addresses two much more recent historical debates: first, the debate regarding the medium specificity of cinema as a new medium (often fought in opposition to other, more established art forms in the first three decades of the twentieth century); second, the contemporary debate regarding the possibilities of cinema or theatre to create the most satisfyingly authentic feeling of presence.

An example of this conflict between media can be found in Balázs's writings from the 1920s, when cinema was not yet considered an art form in its own right. According to Balázs, films were sometimes simply 'photographed theatre', whereas the aim of the filmmaker ought to have been to create a new art form, one that differed from theatre. While in the early days of cinema it was essential to differ from the popular spectacles of vaudeville in order to be considered art, contemporary cinema needs to be something else and something more than a Hollywood franchise to be taken seriously by critics.

It is not difficult to identify a comparable competition between the arts in *Birdman*, and at one significant point, Riggan (the movie star) and Mike (the stage actor) quite literally get into a fight. However, another scene – where they meet on stage and Mike takes over as the director – can also be seen as a battle between the arts, though a different kind of fight, fought with different means. Here, in a battle that seems to be an allegorical, paragonal struggle, it is the actor with greater skills, the one who can remember many lines of script and who knows how to perform live on stage, the actor-with-a-capital-A, who prevails. The winner of the paragone is clearly the theatre actor. The symbolic elements of this corporeal fight, and the more symbolic battle between acting capacities, are supported by other elements of the film, for instance the fact that when specific film actors are mentioned, they are all linked to contemporary blockbusters (such as *The Avengers*) with low cultural status, whereas theatre actors are admired, albeit as ghosts, through tradition and quality (reflected in the way Mike foregrounds that Brando, Hayes and Robards have played on the same stage as he). The modern hype of social media and YouTube fame is depicted as an additional decline in our mediated society. All in all, the film, as Richard Brody, film critic of the *New Yorker*, formulates it, enforces the theme of 'the higher artistic dignity of acting in the theatre' (Brody 2014).

It is, consequently, tempting to end our analysis of *Birdman* on the clear-cut dichotomy of cinema versus theatre, with theatre as the symbolic winner. But even if the film seems to ascribe higher value to the art of theatre performance than movie acting, we don't see the two forms in opposition, but rather as intricately woven (inter)media forms. In this we follow André Bazin, who claims that theatre and film represent 'two different psychological forms of performed entertainment':

> Theatre is built on actors' and viewers' mutual awareness for the other's presence, but with the goal of 'play acting' ... In film, however, the situation is different. There, hidden in a darkened room, we contemplate through partly-opened blinds a performance in the outside world which knows not of our existence. Nothing stands in the way of our imaginary identification with this world in motion before us, which becomes *the* world.
>
> (Bazin 2009b)

In his description of the differences between the art forms, Bazin goes on to point out that cinema can exist without an actor, whereas theatre cannot. And we can be even more precise: when it comes to theatre, it is the role and function of space that is pivotal, or as Frisvold Hanssen puts it:

> Bazin emphasizes the importance of a specific dramatic *space*, of architecture, of the division presented spatially (albeit in different forms throughout theatre history) between the stage and the audience, relating to the audience and demonstratively existing in contrast to the rest of the world.
>
> (Hanssen 2013b)

It is, among other things, in this light that *Birdman* becomes photographed theatre or, perhaps better, *cinematic theatre*, but not in the negative sense that Balázs described. The way we see it, theatre becomes magnified by the film medium, more specifically the photographic images, and the physical and material quality of theatre becomes visible in a different way than within the theatre itself. To be in St James Theatre through the camera is to be present in a way that is at the same time different from and similar to being in the physical theatre ourselves. By being theatrical cinema, *Birdman* also draws attention to cinema, and the multiple ways cinema can interact with other art forms.

Conclusion

In this chapter we have discussed how *Birdman*, by way of the possibilities inherent in cinema, creates a theatrical presence. When it comes to the medialities represented in the film we have, even more so than in the other chapters in this book, had to limit ourselves. Due to Iñárritu's well-known maximalistic approach to filmmaking, the amount of and variation in references is overwhelming. Accordingly, the scenes we have chosen to discuss in detail, and the themes we have chosen to discuss, do not cover everything, far from it. We could have used *Birdman* to discuss music in film, the role of the art critic, as well as social media, in much more detail than we have done, and other readings could easily have demonstrated that *Birdman* shares similarities with films as diverse as *Citizen Kane* and *Louder Than Bombs*, which must be the subject of other engagements with the film. Let us conclude by noting, simply, that Iñárritu and Lubezki had to go to extremes when it came to planning and creating what may seem to be the simplest task of all: producing a feeling of presence.

3.2 The Batman franchise

Birdman's voice is a reference to Michael Keaton's voice as Batman (*Batman* 1989), but as it is even darker and more distinct than Keaton's impersonation of the superhero, it also has clear connotations of the voice of Christian Bale as Batman. The Batman franchise was first created in 1939, and tells the story of Bruce Wayne – billionaire by day, superhero crime fighter by night. It is generally considered to be the most important superhero storyline. Aside from the comics published by DC comics, the 1960s television series (featuring Adam West as Batman), the animated series made for Fox in the 1990s, and the series of feature films based on the comics, are important parts of the franchise. Michael Keaton played Batman in the two first of Warner Brothers's adaptations (*Batman* 1989 and *Batman Returns* 1992, both of which were directed by Tim Burton), but he was later replaced by Val Kilmer and George Clooney. The series was rebooted by Christopher Nolan, who directed three movies about Batman (2005–12) featuring Christian Bale as the superhero.

Notes

1. The short story is also the title of a collection of Raymond Carver's short stories from 1981.
2. For Best Film, Best Director, Best Screenplay and Best Cinematography (Emmanuel Luzbeki). Emmanuel Lubezki is considered to be one of the most innovative cinematographers in contemporary Hollywood cinema, most famous for his collaboration with Iñárritu and Alfonso Cuarón. He also won an Academy Award for *Gravity* (2013) and for *The Revenant* (2015), which makes him the only cinematographer to win three years in a row.
3. The design of this title sequence is clearly inspired by the title sequence in Jean-Luc Godard's *Pierrot Le Fou* (1965), where the letters also appear in alphabetical order. *https://www.youtube.com/watch?v=-717PTVBCdw*
4. On Carver and *Birdman* see Chilton 2015.
5. The complexity of shooting such a scene – including the fact that the producers needed to ask for permission to use the neon signs in the shoot – is described in Gray (2015).
6. See Bruhn (2016b) for an intermedial reading of Carver's short story *Cathedral.*
7. See for instance Harvey (2010). See also Carver's original version of the story with the title *Beginners*, as compared to the edited version (Carver 2007).
8. But also, of course, the film reflects on other films about theatre production such as George Cukor's *A Double Life* (1947) or *Opening Night* (1977).
9. See Isaacs (2016) for a longer ideological discussion of the role of the long-take in Cuarón and Lubezki's films.
10. See *New York Times* video on the anatomy of a scene https://www.youtube.com/watch?v=PVmaJAmQ3yQ (last accessed 30 December 2017).
11. See this illuminating video essay on the long take in Steven Spielberg's films https://www.youtube.com/watch?v=8q4X2vDRfRk (last accessed 30 December 2017).

4 A Novelist on Film? Joachim Trier's *Louder Than Bombs*

When Joachim Trier's third film, *Louder Than Bombs*, was selected to compete for the Palme d'Or at the 2015 Cannes Film Festival, it was considered a major step forward for both the acclaimed indie director and the small film nation of Norway.[1] While his two previous films, *Reprise* (2006) and *Oslo, August 31st* (2011), and his latest, *Thelma* (2017), all are set in Norway, Trier's first English-language film was international in its setting, style and its strong cast, featuring Isabelle Huppert, Gabriel Byrne and Jesse Eisenberg. Stylistically as well as thematically, *Louder Than Bombs* can be considered an amalgamation of European and American filmmaking. Trier and scriptwriter Eskil Vogt, his long-time collaborator, combine narrative elements from European modernism with the American family drama tradition, focusing specifically on the theme of mourning.[2]

The film depicts an American east-coast family comprising father Gene (Byrne), a former actor turned high school teacher, and his two sons. Jonah (Eisenberg) is around 30 and teaches sociology at a university in another state; Conrad (Devin Druid) lives with Gene and is a student at the high school where he works. Their mother was the world-famous press photographer Isabelle Reed (Isabelle Huppert), who died three years before the story takes place. A significant exhibition of her work is being planned, and in relation to this, her journalist colleague (and, as we learn, former lover) Richard Weissman (David Straitharn) is about to write a feature story on her work. The story will include the truth about her death: that what appeared to be a car accident was in fact suicide, something that has been kept secret from the youngest son, Conrad. Gene and Conrad have a troubled relationship, and when Jonah comes home immediately after his wife has given birth to their child, the atmosphere becomes tense. The possible beginning of a fragile, amorous connection between Conrad and Melanie, a girl from his class (Ruby Jerins), offers new life experiences to the introverted boy. The film ends on a relatively optimistic note of hope and unity in the wounded family.

Stylistically, the film operates with a fractured chronology, but despite the complex narration (including a number of flashbacks, dream sequences and repetitions of the same scenes from different points of view), the seamless editing actually gives an impression of a relatively straightforward story, an impression helped along by the refined sound and music design. The beautifully controlled cinematic style is contemplative, almost subdued, and creates the feeling, despite the experimental aspects of the film, of a more traditional, character-based family drama.

Reception and general background

Louder Than Bombs is Trier's most underestimated film. The Swedish newspaper *Svenska Dagbladet* – reflecting, more or less, the general trend in the Scandinavian reception – regarded *Louder Than Bombs* as a film that, under the guise of direct storytelling, 'touches upon life's big questions: life and death, sincerity and deception, introvertedness and extrovertedness, communication and silence.' Furthermore, the reviewer described it as 'exquisitely filmed and incredibly well acted, all the way through' (Hellsten 2015). On a similar note, Norwegian paper *VG* described the film as 'a particularly ambitious, existential drama', in a review that underlined a theme that we, too, shall discuss in detail: 'the problems inherent in human communication' (Selås 2015). But rather than consider this in the light of the heavy presence of medialities in the film, the reviewer focused on the film's existential themes: the film investigates 'how we can become estranged from people close to ourselves and thus from ourselves'. Another reviewer, from American *Variety*, touches upon the arts and medialities, namely 'the issue of artistic ambition [of Isabelle Reed] and how committing to a creative career (or abandoning it, as the case may be) shapes our lives and the relationships we maintain with loved ones' (Debruge 2015).

Existential and psychological themes were consistently foregrounded in the reception of the film, with Norwegian critic Dag Sødtholt's detailed analysis of its structural and narratological complexities in online film journal *Montages* as a notable exception (Sødtholt 2016). Overall, both in Scandinavia and internationally, the film received positive if not over-enthusiastic reviews, probably because it was regarded in the genre-frame of family drama.[3] Indeed, *Louder Than Bombs* does depict and discuss distress and trauma within the framework of a family, and thus relates to the tradition of dramas such as *Ice Storm* (Ang Lee 1997), *The Sweet Hereafter* (Atom Egoyan 1997), *Ordinary People* (Robert Redford 1980), as well as its contemporary, *Manchester by the Sea* (Kenneth Lonergran 2016).

In terms of structure, the film has an opening that is conspicuously devoid of media: the sequence after the mandatory company logos, but before the presentation of the title, consists of four minutes of extremely intimate cinematic images, almost exaggeratedly freed from any medialities. This sequence begins with an extreme close-up of a young man (Jonah) and his new-born daughter, followed by intimate conversations between the new parents in hushed voices in low volume. This is followed by the almost ironically forceful, sound-related title *Louder*

Than Bombs. From this point on, the narrative jumps forward in time, but contains numerous flashbacks and dream sequences. Thematically and psychologically, the film offers a heart-breaking portrait of a family living through a critical moment, three years after the death of the mother. The father, although wanting to do his best, is unable to relate to his sons in a satisfactory manner. His oldest son cannot come to terms with his new role as a father, and finds himself lying and running away from his new responsibilities, while not hesitating to advise and even judge his father and his brother, who, like his father and himself, lives under the spell of the death of his mother in addition to suffering the well-known miseries of teenage life.

The opening scene initiates the thematic core that the critics have almost unanimously focused on: the dichotomy between emotional presence and absence, and particularly the underlying risk of lies finding their way into our most intimate relations. It echoes or corresponds with the final scenes of the film, with the family, reunited (the dead mother imaginarily present) in the car with the father and his two sons. Like the opening, this last scene has an almost non-media pureness. No mobile phones or cameras, no books or music in the car (only the discreet extradiegetic musical sound support, which also accompanies Conrad's voice-over description of an important dream earlier in the film): just human beings together in the car's narrow space, seemingly in no need of any mediating devices, not even their own voices. But in-between these two media-less scenes, the film is literally filled with media occurrences, and it is the presence and function of, and internal relations between, these that we are interested in investigating.

We want to argue that the film's somewhat lukewarm reception might be the result of the reviewers' lack of interest in the presence and function of medialities, and we wish to demonstrate that different technical and qualified media play crucial roles both aesthetically and thematically. However, as foregrounded by the jury for the Nordic Council Film prize, the richness of the film should 'ensure its place in the curriculum of film schools around the world' (2016). While the jury in particular praise the complexity of the film's storytelling we will look at the crucial aspects of mediation in the film.

In *Louder Than Bombs*, we see exemplified the double aspect of media: on one hand media as a bridge between people, and on the other as a hindrance to people meeting and communicating. Consequently, we want to understand the film not so much as a family drama, but rather as a 'medialities drama', to coin a new, awkward cinematic sub-generic label. When we investigate the existential themes in the light of the complex constellation of medialities in the film, new perspectives become illuminated. We will demonstrate how the well-known literary genre of the *Künstlerroman* (in which the novel depicts how (usually) a young man becomes an artist)[4] is investigated and used in a particular way in this film. From this analysis, we can see that, although it possesses eminently cinematic qualities, lauded by many critics, Trier's film also shares deep affinities with novelistic discourse. Literature and novelistic form is not only a theme particularly tied to Conrad as a budding *Künstler*, there are crucial elements both in the film's content and in its form that could be understood as novelistic devices.

We investigate this by way of the three-step model consisting of cataloguing, structuring and contextualising, as sketched in the Introduction.

Step one: cataloguing medialities in *Louder Than Bombs*

As a first step toward understanding *Louder Than Bombs* as a reflection and discussion of medialities (and, consequently, as a *Künstlerroman*), an overview of the categories of medialities represented in the film is necessary. Following our earlier definitions, we distinguish between media that are represented mainly by way of either their technical or by their qualified (often aesthetic) dimension.

Starting with the qualified media dimension, it feels natural to begin with photography, which relates to major thematic clusters in the film. Photography is thematically crucial in *Louder Than Bombs* because the deceased Isabelle Reed was a famous war photographer. It is implied that Gene and Isabelle met when he had his headshot taken by her. Throughout *Louder Than Bombs*, photography is represented in different forms: as negatives in plastic charteques, as small paper copies, as files on a digital memory stick, as images on computer screens, as large exhibition objects, and as still images from a documentary film within the film. Photography works as news reporting, it works scientifically, as an X-ray, ceremonially, at the funeral, and as documentation, when proud grandfather Gene shows Jonah's new-born off to his colleagues on his mobile phone. In other words, the presence of photography in the film mirrors the role of photography in the lives of people today, for instance in our Facebook feeds. Not only do we see others and the world through photography, we tend to even see ourselves through images (photographic or not), as noted by Roland Barthes (Barthes 1981).

The very first time Isabelle Reed is introduced to us, it is through a documentary film honouring her as photographer, a parallel to Orson Welles's introduction of his main, dead character through a newsreel at the beginning of *Citizen Kane* (see Chapter 2). The documentary is in itself a complex mixture of different components: Isabelle's own voice-overs, comments from her colleague (and lover) Richard, her own photographs, authentic footage from different warzones, scenes with her in warzones, a video recording from an award ceremony where she was honoured for her work, an interview with her from real American talk show *Charlie Rose*. The documentary stands out from the rest of the film, because while it plays into the existential themes of the film, it does this in a particularly media-saturated way.

Photography is by far the most represented and discussed mediality of the film, but other qualified media occur and have important functions in *Louder Than Bombs* too. Another qualified mediality that is discretely present throughout the film is news media (partial news clips in the documentary about Isabelle, news coverage of the war in Afghanistan, the front-page story about Isabelle in the *New York Times*). Music is present in a psychologically characterising function – we see Conrad constantly listening to music on his headphones wherever he is – but also as a qualified mediality through the electronic dance music he puts on when he (to his brother's surprise) is dancing alone in his room (making dance yet another qualified, communicative form for Conrad). We also encounter music in his dream where he finds Melanie lying on the ground in the forest. Conrad's room is decorated with his own drawings, and one of his earlier ones, depicting his mother's near-fatal accident, is given to her as a present. Computer games are another mediality intimately tied to Conrad (also tried out, without luck, by his father), as are YouTube-videos (including clips from films such as Dario Argento's horror classic *Opera*, from 1987) and Google searches. This is all described in Conrad's own media text, which we shall return to. Conrad also watches clips from his father's acting career on YouTube, and shares a soap-opera clip he discovers with his brother.

Finally, we have a large group that we might call the 'literature' cluster, which comprises a number of instances. The most important are: a novel being read aloud in class; Conrad's own writings that he shows to his brother; a completed manuscript he later delivers to Melanie's house; Melanie's extradiegetic, literary sounding voice-over towards the end of the film. We will return to this literary cluster and the remediation of literature by way of voice-over later.

Technical media dimensions are also important, for instance in the different devices playing a part in the representation of photography: the camera, the memory-cards, the negatives in Isabelle's darkroom/atelier, and the computer on which Jonah views and later deletes the photos disclosing the affair between Richard and Isabelle (Figure 4.1).

Figure 4.1 Photography as involuntary disclosure: photo of Isabelle in a private, and even secret setting.

Another technical mediality is the telephone, which plays various plot-important roles and which is probably the best example of the intricate doubleness of mediality creating both bridges and barriers that we return to below.

This rudimentary registration of represented medialities makes us, if nothing else, aware that this is indeed a media-saturated film. Apart from the intro scene (with Jonah intensely interacting with his new-born child) and the final scene (with Gene, Conrad and Jonah silently riding the car), qualified and technical medialities are, literally, everywhere. Either simply present or, in many instances, explicitly part of plot-producing events. All major characters relate to media in some way, and all important discussions between the characters spring from questions that are either related to or directly produced by medialities.

Step two: structuring medialities in *Louder Than Bombs*

Following our heteromedial point of departure, the observation that *the film is full of medialities* seems trivial: media are per definition mixed, the question should always be 'What does this mixture mean, what function does it have?' From an analytical point of view, we must ask in what ways the analytical focus on media opens up new and interesting questions.

When trying to structure the media-related material, it once again becomes evident that the film explores much more than just family relations. Another central theme is the question of identity, and particularly identity as a product of mediation. This theme is present in a scene in the film which, typically, is both imbedded in the family drama structure but also drenched in mediality representations: Jonah is helping his father sort through the photographic archive of his deceased mother, a project prompted by the memorial exhibition at an art gallery. For the family, and Jonah in particular, who had an almost erotically charged relation with his mother (this is strongly implied in a sequence where Isabelle visits him at his college), it is important to edit the collection before the exhibition. During this work, Conrad finds an old photo of his father from his acting days (Figure 4.2) and, laughing, shows it to his

Figure 4.2 Gene's head shot as a young actor.

brother, who says: 'We wouldn't want this to fall into the wrong hands, would we? [. . .] What *are* we even looking at here?'

Jonah then mimics an imaginary casting agent filling a role based on this particular photo: 'Yes, we would like him'. Jonah, Conrad and even Gene laugh until Gene shows them the back of the photo, with Isabelle's signature and professional photographer's stamp. The scene suggests that this was how they met, she as a photographer, he as the object of her work: 'She kept it because she thought it was a really good photo of me', says Gene.

Beneath the intricate emotional and existential familial knots being tied and untied here, this scene also investigates what images and photos *do* in our lives and what an image is. Photographs are present in the lives of all people in the western world today, and we use them mostly without thinking about their medium characteristics. Despite this, they are closely related to our private and public identity. We use photographs in our passports, to identify ourselves, and we share images in which we look our best on Instagram, Snapchat or Facebook. Do the images we post online really represent our true selves? Can we trust the images that we encounter to give a true impression of who others are? In intermedial terms this leads to a host of related questions concerning a priori connections to the other medialities we listed in step 1.

Thus, *Louder Than Bombs* is preoccupied with questions of what an image is and whether an image is able to convey the truth of the identity of a person.[5] Trier and Vogt foreground this by constantly reminding us that images are mediated, and that they need to move through the materialised bodies of technical media in order to reach us.

4.1 Roland Barthes, studium and punctum

Roland Barthes has described some of the forms in which images in general and photos in particular are part of our lives. (See also our discussion of the functions of photography in Chapter 4.) He famously distinguished between two approaches to photography: as *studium* or *punctum*. Studium is our way of approaching images politely, in a distanced manner, as in academic work where we apply analytical and intellectual tools. Punctum marks the inverse opposite; the punctum aspects of images strike our individual experiences of the present or the past. Journalistic photography (Figure 4.3) is most often studium related, which is why we are able to carelessly scroll through terrible news images: 'In these images, *no punctum*: a certain shock – the literal can traumatize – but no disturbance; the photograph can 'shout,' not wound' (Barthes 1981). Like the man that Isabelle passes by in a scene in the film who just leafs through the *New York Times* copy (Figure 4.4), we may browse these images in a disengaged manner, but we do not find the detail that hooks us.

But, and this is even more important in relation to *Louder Than Bombs*, according to Barthes, photography has a peculiar ability to offer presence in time. Barthes's *Camera Lucida* was written after the loss of his mother, and the medium specificity of photography, its ability to make present again that which has been but exists no longer, is demonstrated through the lens of the author's mourning (Barthes 1981).

Figure 4.3 Photography as punctum. *Louder than Bombs* represents a photo representing a photo: woman with an image of her dead son.

Figure 4.4 The everyday use (or negligence) of photography in the news stream.

This 'active' function of photography (as opposed to an understanding of photography as mere representation) is important in *Louder Than Bombs*, where the deceased Isabelle is present only through photographs and the traumatised memories these evoke, and it becomes a crucial point for the film that a photograph (and really, any media product) is always defined by the perspective from which it was taken and the framing this perspective produces (Figure 4.5). Conrad, in his text,

Figure 4.5 Isabelle's official portrait photo used in the film about her.

describes how his mother taught him about framing and perspective, and as a kind of echo of this we see the same situation (Conrad's loneliness after school) from both his father's and his own perspective.

However, the theme of photography and the question of the 'right' or 'good' picture of someone may be understood in a larger, general intermedial or media theoretical context we could call media opening lines of communication or closing gateways, a dichotomy briefly discussed in the Introduction. As seen from the description above, photography creates *both* closeness and distance in this film.

But the medialities, as they are represented in specific scenes in the film, may be divided into *media that bring people together* (including the scenes where no technical media come between people) – *or media that keep people apart. Louder Than Bombs* is consequently not only a film about (troubled) relations between people/family, it is very much a film about the relationship between human beings and media. Media may facilitate meetings, such as when Jonah and Conrad are having fun with old, embarrassing clips of their dad, or when they play computer games together. The computer as a technical medium on which Jonah skypes with his wife is a bridge between human beings. Conrad has learned to express himself through music and drawings (among these, a self-portrait on his wall), and he feels that his films (both DVDs and films on his computer) and books contain important psychological and existential lessons for him.

However, it is characteristic of *Louder Than Bombs* that several of the media are *both* communicative hindrances *and* communicative possibilities. Maybe the most illustrative case here is the mobile phone, which we understand as primarily a technical medium: while Gene is attempting to get in touch with his son on the phone, Conrad can choose to close the conversation or not even answer the call (which is the case when he spends the night out and his father is worried). The music in Conrad's headphones works as a barrier between him and other people (but his music at one point attracts Jonah, and thus opens up their relation), and is perhaps the most unambiguously non-social medium in the film. Conrad's obsession with computer games is mostly on the side of solipsism, it is a lonely life in a virtual world (with only virtual co-players), and Trier seems to underline this point in almost parodic terms when Gene, in an attempt to connect with his hostile and absent son (connect online, that is) engages in learning how to play the game *The Elder Scrolls* online. Gene's well-meaning but clandestine strategy is risky, though, and when he is finally supposed to *meet* Conrad in the virtual reality of the game, in his avatar disguise, Conrad resolutely kills him, without ever knowing that he is slaying his own father.[6] This scene can nonetheless be read as quite positive towards computer games as a medium and practice; like literature, the computer game allows Conrad to express his feelings (here his hatred towards his father) in a way that he may not, to the same extent, in other areas of his life, and as such, through the other media he engages with. Read in this light, the computer game is as expressive, and perhaps as liberating, as literature. In his own writing, Conrad describes how he enjoys changing between different avatars and how being different persons gives him access to different skills. Conrad's computer games could also be compared with Isabelle's photography.[7] This all forms a neat parallel to Isabelle's dangerous but also exciting life as a war photographer. For a long while, the spectator is actively, through the film's narrative devices, lead to believe that Conrad is deeply miserable, perhaps even approaching depression and a potential violent outburst, an assumption shared by his brother, who at one point in the middle of the film asks him: 'You are not gonna shoot up a school, are you?'

4.2 Joachim Trier's short movies

A marked interest in the relationship between different visually orientated media was obvious in Trier's short films from his years at film school: *Pieta* (2000) opens with a photo of a child and the adult narrator claiming that 'The first thing I remember is that my mother took a picture of me'. *Still* (2001) deals with a dying film photographer's retrospective on his life, composed of both moving and still images; in *Proctor* (2002) the protagonist witnesses a suicide, which is also recorded on video, a recording he watches again and again, and the feature film *Oslo, August 31st* opens with a number of auditive memories structured by the repeated phrase 'I remember' combined with archival pictures of Oslo from the 1970s and 80s.

But, compared to the world of photography, music and computer games, which are all related to both opening as well as closing doors between people, there is one mediality in the film that consistently opens views and creates new understandings and reactivates memories, and that medium is literature. In the comprehensive system of represented medialities in *Louder Than Bombs*, literature is the medium invested with the most hopeful energy.

Before we analyse the presence of literature as a qualified medium in the film, let us stress that in this specific context we understand literature as the aesthetically formed verbal representation of reality (as opposed to ordinary verbal conversations in the film, or the written verbal communication that we encounter as part of the computer games and the newspaper material).

We meet literature initially in the classroom scene, where a story is being read out loud by Melanie.[8] Then we have Conrad's autobiographical writing, which he shows to his brother on his computer. The third instance is when we see him writing, and the fourth when we encounter this same text in the form of the written material he has printed out and hands over to Melanie at her house. Finally, the fifth time the film uses literature is towards the end, when the actor playing Melanie again reads aloud on voice-over. In this voice-over, the episode that takes place on-screen is being narrated from the perspective of a third person looking back at this from a future point in time, leaving the impression that this is actually Conrad's writing. These four instances of literature are installed at four relatively regularly spaced-out moments of the film and as such offer a kind of supporting, underlying structure for the film, hidden as it may be. In the following, we comment on these scenes, below numbered 1–5.

1. The classroom scene

The classroom scene offers a first insight into Conrad's inner life; we get a glimpse into his rich reflections and feelings, and Trier and Vogt manage to show us this in a highly sophisticated way. *First*, and this is pretty direct, by letting the spectator understand that the text being read out in class resonates with Conrad's own inner emotions (Conrad feels that the text he hears is 'about him'): this indicates that an author may actually communicate something in aesthetic terms that directly speaks to a reader. And *secondly*, that the words, memories and dreams and hopes have become Conrad's own: the film seems to say that Conrad has turned the literary experience into his own, that he appropriates the literary discourse for his own purposes. We see, in other words, a two-step process: first the strong, general identification, then a personal, intimate appropriation of the text. It is worth noting that this all takes place in the form of a curious mixture of diegetic loud-reading in the classroom and a voice-over following Conrad's stream of consciousness, the borders or limits of both of which are hard to establish. Trier did something similar with great effect in his debut film, *Reprise*, and co-writer Eskil

Vogt used comparable techniques in *Blind* (2014), but it is typical of *Louder Than Bombs*, as compared to these other examples, that rather than create an effect of *Verfremdung* (as the voice-over effects in Trier's earlier film did), the editing and sound effects here create a seemingly perfect continuity, and blur the distinction between the outside world and subjective imagery rather than exhibit it.

2. Autobiographical writing

This identification/appropriation leads – with a 'delay' of around twenty-five minutes, to the next 'literary' scene in the film, where we receive more direct access to Conrad's mind. This scene (which we will return to in the concluding section of this chapter) takes place just after a scene that constitutes a classical medial paragone situation, that is, a competition between the arts or media: in a rather arrogant and didactic way, Jonah 'teaches' Conrad about the false truth claims of computer games, and as a kind of reply to this, Conrad (courageously) shows Jonah his own writings (Figure 4.6). We access his own content and form, without the mediation of another author's word.

Jonah reads Conrad's text on his brother's computer screen, but the viewer gets access to it by way of Conrad reading it aloud in a voice-over (all but the very first sentences), and the text consists of an idiosyncratic and original mixture of dreams, reminiscences, dry facts and curious observations and everyday occurrences.

The literary style is a paratactic first-person narration, where details (how many socks in his drawer) and existential issues (concerning death in particular) stand side by side. The ending is highly significant: he mentions a lesson his mother taught him that had a 'profound effect' on him, namely that it is the *framing* (not the motif in itself) that produces

Figure 4.6 Conrad's gaming; the qualified medium of computer games as mediated through the technical medium of the computer screen.

the full meaning of a given image.[9] Conrad's text is accompanied or illustrated by a stream of images from a number of different sources: his own life, his computer games, YouTube, etc. This creates an upbeat, visual stream-of-consciousness, made up of both words and images, that is highly complex and yet easy to follow, and which provides, as mentioned, a fascinating view inside the subjective life of Conrad. And we learn that his inner life is deeply influenced by the medialities he passively consumes and actively uses. We see that he is of course deeply marked by the death of his mother, and a crucial theme connecting parts of the text and images in this phenomenal sequence is death and decay. But at the same time, his inner life is revealed to be original and passionate: this is *not* the weak-willed and passive inner life of the depressed man Trier has portrayed in his earlier works (particularly in, *Oslo, August 31st*).

Depression in *Louder Than Bombs* is instead the burden of the middle-aged woman, not really the issue of the young man (although Jonah is definitely low in the film), and we (contrary to his father, Gene) do not feel that Conrad is a teenager in danger of turning his despair into violence or destruction, like those portrayed in in *Elephant* (Gus van Sant 2003) or *We Need to Talk About Kevin* (Lynne Ramsay 2011).[10]

3. *Writing scene*

This is a brief scene, less than 10 seconds, squeezed in between yet another difficult quarrel between Conrad and his father, and the memory of one of the dangerous work-accidents of his mother, presumably the one that led her to quit her travels in war zones thus indirectly leading to her depression and suicide in the US. Conrad is sitting in his dark room, as when he is playing computer games, but instead he is writing, intensely concentrated.

4. *Handing over the manuscript to Melanie*

Because of the general kaleidoscopic chronology of *Louder Than Bombs*, it is somewhat difficult to pin down the exact time of the next literary incident in the film, when Conrad – despite his brother's advice not to show his writing to Melanie – leaves a print-out of his work on her doorstep, after a very brief scene where we see him starting to print the text. We later learn that she does not even know his name, but Conrad handing his material over to her is still a crucial turning point in his life. We understand this by watching his face: when running home from Melanie's house he has, almost for the first time in the entire film, a huge grin on his face. In other words, literature is not actually mentioned or seen in this scene, but we see that writing literature, and daring to share it with others (and thus exposing oneself) has possible healing effects.

5. 'Melanie' reciting from the manuscript

The fifth and final 'literary' scene is as paradoxical as the first one, in which the voice of Melanie suddenly starts expressing the inner feelings of Conrad. But here, although Melanie is still the reader, the prose is markedly different. Not only is it written in the past tense, giving the narrator the perspective of hindsight, it is also written in the third person, although representing distinctly the experience and knowledge of Conrad. Furthermore, the style is no longer an immediate paratactic stream of consciousness, but a much more deliberate, well-argued creative prose; we get the impression that this is the work of a much more mature, maybe published writer, a feeling that is helped along by the way Melanie reads it, in a much more self-confident and rhythmic manner. (And the 'literary' style of the voice-over here is what distinguishes it from the final and much more immediate and direct verbal style of the Conrad's voice-over in the final dream-scene in the film, where it is the contents of the dream that are described.)

From the point of view of the technical media dimension of literature (i.e. which technical devices mediate the literature), we observe a certain system: from (1), the 'immaterial' reception of literature in Conrad's thought, moving over to (2), the digitalised text (perhaps here still functioning as a less 'material' version of writing) on the interface of his computer, leading to (3), the more markedly tactile and material, printed version of his work that he gives to Melanie, which – but now we speculate – may indicate the future existence of a real, printed 'book' of Conrad's writings. That is, we observe a gradual move from immaterial to material aspects in the technical mediation of literature. Thematically, this makes it possible to read the four literary scenes as a narrative depicting a development in Conrad, starting with his experience of the intersubjective possibilities of literature in the classroom scene, before moving into his original, if also rather embryonic, paratactic 'list' of important issues and observations from his life, which he has the courage and initiative to give to his attractive but probably also unattainable classmate Melanie. A narrative that ends with his more accomplished literary text, which manages to put his complex and emotionally difficult experiences into well-structured and aesthetically pleasing prose.

As compared to the more radical style of Trier's and Vogt's use of the device in earlier work, in *Louder Than Bombs* Trier manages to use the voice-over more subtly, which produces an effect of personal multiplicity, at the same time complex and discrete. Isabelle, Gene, Conrad and Melanie are all present as voices in the film's voice-over: Isabelle is heard describing her photographs, as well as the experience of being torn between her work and her private life; Gene's voice is an internal voice, in which he comments on his behaviour when he meets Hannah for the first time; Conrad gives words and voice to a dream about his whole family, including Jonah's newborn baby in the shape of an old man; Melanie vocalises what we think is Conrad's story. Vogt and Trier's insistence on the use and investigation of voice-overs can be related to another highly characteristic trait of *Louder Than Bombs*, namely its complex narrative structure. The film revels in flashbacks, different perspectives, and flashbacks within flashbacks, all of which come together to produce an unusually elaborate and intricate temporal and perspectival cinematic form.

Summing up step two

The voice-over and the complicated temporal and perspectival form are, we believe, important signs of not only a literary but more specifically a novelistic tendency in this film. Furthermore, the role of literature is prominent in the plot, particularly as it relates to the portrait of the main protagonist Conrad. The role of literature can also be described using the intermedial term 'formal imitation'. As described in the Introduction, this term denotes that formal aspects of a media product are mimicking the central formal attributes of another mediality. So when we claim that we understand the film as a novelistic film, it does not only refer to the fact that it is possible to read the aesthetic development of the protagonist Conrad – following the pattern of the *Künstlerroman* – as a road towards creating a kind of novel inside the diegetic level of the film, but also that the entire structuring of the film imitates central aspects of novelistic discourse, particularly the form and content of the high modernist novel as we know it.[11] The high modernist novel, investigating existential and psychological themes, offered new and, to many, highly alienating takes on chronological structure; it questioned the nature of space and place and pointed to entirely new ways of understanding and representing the inner workings and perceptual mechanisms of individual human beings.

In other words, and this we see as the result of the second step of the analysis: the film creates a paradoxical intermedial position which relates to the age-old paragone debate, and it does so in a curious way, namely by implicitly showing, in form and in content, that its highest aim is to resemble a novel. Or more precisely, in this, in many ways highly satisfactory, cinematic form, the film approaches and even imitates crucial aspects of what could be defined as novelistic style. This idea has already been hinted at by David Thomson in *The Guardian's* film blog, where he briefly implies such a reading. Thompson applauds Jesse Eisenberg's performance saying that his face 'is a model for the novelistic depth [that] movie acting can convey in 10 seconds, or less', and he concludes his piece by stating that Trier is 'a novelist on film' (Thomson 2016).

Step three: framing the structured medialities in *Louder Than Bombs*

In the last and concluding step of the intermedial three-step model, different framings or contextualisations are brought into play to suggest ways of interpreting the analytical endeavours of the two previous steps. Possible contexts can be socio-historical aspects that relate to the intermedial relations, aesthetic or philosophical theories, biographical background or genre related issues – or a combination of some or all of these that helps explain not only the presence but also the function of medialities inside the text. In this particular case, it might have been rewarding to compare *Louder Than Bombs* more methodically with the genre of family drama. Such a comparison could explain the new, to Trier, and more mainstreamed cinematic style, including an international cast of actors. From a more media-centric point of view, the presence and function of photography, which serves both as a plot element and an important part of the medial economy of the film, could also be further examined. However, we will suggest another context, namely Trier's earlier work, upon the scaffold of which we will construct an explanation of some of the central findings of the intermedial analysis of *Louder Than Bombs*.

Let us first recapitulate the results of this chapter so far. We have repeatedly argued against understanding *Louder Than Bombs* solely as a family drama – without denying that it is indeed a film about family, specifically a traumatised family grieving the loss of the mother. We found, initially and on a very general level, that the film contains an unusually rich presence of media (demonstrated in step one). In step two we argued that in a dichotomy between literature and film, literature, and more specifically novelistic form, became an implicit aesthetic ideal, directly related to an important generic plot structure supporting the film – the developmental *Künstlerroman*.

In this third, framing step, we will argue that a useful gateway to understanding this intense interest in literature, and specifically the novelistic as an aesthetic ideal, is to relate *Louder Than Bombs* to Trier's and his co-creator Eskil Vogt's earlier works. These include Vogt's *Blind* and Trier's *Oslo, August 31st* (2011) (also about a (former) writer), but our focus will be on Trier's *Reprise* (2006). This comparison will put into perspective and partly explain the deep and multifaceted literary affinities we have demonstrated in *Louder Than Bombs*.

Trier's debut feature film *Reprise*, co-written with Eskil Vogt, is in several ways indebted to the French modernist auteur tradition that Trier has repeatedly referred to as one of the main inspirations for his work. *Reprise* is about two young men and their parallel but very different attempts at breaking through as writers in Norway. On one hand, the film offers a contemporary, Norwegian version of the emotional sincerity found in Truffaut's *Jules et Jim* (1962); it creates impact through energetic boosts of humour and a strong sense of identification, without ever failing to confront the tougher and even tragic aspects of artistic ambitions and disappointments combined. As *New York Times* critic Manhola Dargis writes in relation to his debut film: 'I write, therefore I am' (Dargis 2008). On the other hand, *Reprise*, by constructing a system of both chronological and enunciative complexities, develops an artistically playful mode, and thus leans on more intellectualising trends, focused on modernist stylistic experimentation and literary quotation, in French film, closer to the Godard or Resnais style than that of Truffaut. In *Reprise*, Trier and Vogt managed to mix formal experimentation with both tragic and exhilarating scenes, and the film became a national and international critical success.

Apart from 'being about' literature in the sense that it deals with two young writers, *Reprise* can, in its entirety, be considered an example of the intermedial concept of 'formal imitation' already discussed above. It can also, despite its manifestly cinematic qualities, in cinematography and sound design as well as performances, be argued to follow the major traits of what can be defined as the key formal aspects of the high modernist novel as created by Woolf, Joyce and Proust.

One fundamental reason for comparing *Louder Than Bombs* with *Reprise* is to note that we consider *Louder Than Bombs* a less extreme and thus perhaps a more mature version of the debut film. *Louder Than Bombs* definitely experiments with the basics of film language, both when it comes to visual aspects and the sound and voice-over devices discussed above, but the editing and general cinematic style of the film tends to smooth over rather than underline this experimentation.

Louder Than Bombs is not just a modified version of *Reprise*, but we can use this comparison to better understand some of the most interesting – even from an intermedial point of view – aspects of *Louder Than Bombs*. It is particularly illuminating to once again look at the perhaps most impressive scene of the film (a scene also specifically mentioned by multiple reviewers): Conrad's fascinating written narrative that is being 'illustrated'.

The four-minute sequence is a literary mini-narrative steeped in and inspired by contemporary mediascapes, to which it itself contributes. It beautifully captures an upbeat, intense, and formally rewarding version of a young man's attempt to make sense of his own life and the sometimes incomprehensible world surrounding him. The literary attempts of the two young men from *Reprise* are here reorganised into what feels like a more appropriately contemporary form, consisting of personal observations, realistic but seemingly banal lists, quotes from mass media and social media, and traumatic memories or dreams. This sequence, which we described above as one of the four major literature instances in *Louder Than Bombs*, lies *between* the formal and existential questions of this film and *Reprise*. As mentioned above, it is the literary voice-over that produces a kind of cognitive continuity in the sequence; it even makes the flow of images intelligible. Thematically, the sequence clearly fits into *Louder Than Bombs*, but on a formal level it lies closer to the experimental endeavours of *Reprise.*

The mini narrative works as a *mise en abyme* of the entire film's attempt to offer a contemporary version of an existential drama, while also repeating, in a milder fashion, themes and devices from Trier's earlier work. Among what is different, in the mini narrative but also in the film as a whole, from *Reprise*, we can point to the focus on what used to be called new or digital media: games, entertainment and archiving on YouTube, the increased use and, thus, importance of mobile phones – as both communicative devices and cameras providing viral YouTube videos. The comparison with and distinction from *Reprise*, then, can demonstrate how *Louder Than Bombs*, in general and in the four-minute fragment in particular, situates itself in a contemporary world that must necessarily be presented as defined by contemporary media.

Friedrich Kittler famously opened his analysis of what we would call the influence of technical and qualified media on the lives of human beings with the proclamation: 'Media determine our situation' (1999). Trier seems to have moved to a comparable position in his cinema, because an underlying argument in *Louder Than Bombs* is that it is impossible to understand a human being without considering the media with which they live, think, and create. The verbo-visual micro-narrative, apparently fragmented but nonetheless coherent, offers an aesthetically and psychologically satisfying vision of what a highly media-saturated novelistic film language might look like. Additionally, as our reading has shown, the family members in *Louder Than Bombs* all have problems grasping the whole picture on their own, the story about their lives and relations is fragmented, and they are only able to see bits and pieces. While the telephone, the computer and the camera are present, these media are unable to bring together a full picture in the way literature can connect the dots through a young writer's diary, and gather the family as a unit in the end.

Notes

1. *Louder Than Bombs* was the first Norwegian film selected for the competition since Anja Breien's *Arven* in 1979. Norway produces approximately twenty to twenty-five movies a year.
2. For more about Trier's inspirations see Trier (2016).
3. Trier received the Norwegian critics award in 2015 and the Nordic Ministry's film award in 2016. The film has a 78% score on Rotten Tomatoes. While *Sight & Sound* (Roddick 2015) was negative towards the film, *Indiewire* was positive (Kohn 2015), to give a couple of examples.
4. This standard definition of the *Künstlerroman* covers the concept nicely: 'The German term (meaning "artist novel") for a novel in

which the central character is an artist of any kind, e.g. the musical composer Leverkühn in Thomas Mann's *Doktor Faustus* (1947), or the painter Lantier in Zola's *L'Oeuvre* (1886). Although this category of fiction often overlaps with the Bildungsroman in showing the protagonist's development from childhood or adolescence, most famously in Joyce's *A Portrait of the Artist as a Young Man* (1916), it also includes studies of artists in middle or old age, and sometimes of historical persons: in David Malouf's *An Imaginary Life* (1978), for example, the central character and narrator is the Roman poet Ovid (43 BCE–17 CE).'

5. At one point in the film, Conrad visits the graveyard and throws himself on the grave of Carlos Valdez, a clear reference to Carlotta Valdez, the mysterious dead woman in Alfred Hitchcock's *Vertigo* (1956), one of film history's most significant films about loss, truth and identity.
6. The reference to King Oedipus is not hard to detect: Conrad is a slave to his false perceptions, not in the real world, but in the shadow world of digital media, and this leads to his killing of his own father.
7. An illuminating comparison between Conrad's computer games and Isabelle's role as a photographer has been suggested by Dag Sødtholt (2016). Most of all, however, the game constitutes a parallel to his mother's profession: Conrad is immersed in a world torn apart by violence and war, it is addictive, and an environment totally at odds with his suburban surroundings, all of which are features of Isabelle's life as a war photographer.
8. The novel that the students are reading in the classroom is supposedly written by E. I. Lonoff. This is the name of the writer that Philip Roth's alter ego Zuckerman works for in *The Writer.* The text is written by Eskil Vogt (Trier 2017).
9. As such Conrad's written observations and thoughts tap directly into his mother's photographic practice, which was also the immediate preparation of this scene: in a two-minute photo essay Isabelle explained her fundamental thoughts on and problems with photography as a medium and a journalistic practice while some of her own photographs were displayed.
10. It might also be useful to compare with Sarah Polley's documentary from 2012, *Stories We Tell*, which resembles *Louder Than Bombs* in both subject matter (coming to terms with a complicated family story) and form (telling the family story by way of complex twists and turns in perspective, chronology and also technical and qualified medialities).
11. For instance, in the work of Virginia Woolf, James Joyce and Marcel Proust at the beginning of the twentieth century (as well as modernist directors such as Alain Resnais and Nicholas Roeg).

5 Between Cinema and Photography: Jan Troell's *Everlasting Moments*

The photograph shows a young woman, frozen in motion, turning away from the photographer. The viewer, Maria Larsson, stares at her own portrait: 'I cannot make sense of how it happens!' The photographer spots a movement in the air, unscrews the lens from the camera – 'May I ask for your hand' – and holds it up towards the light. The picture of a butterfly is projected onto the inside of Maria's hand (Figure 5.1). The shadow of the butterfly's wings flutters like moving images, within the frame of light, against her palm. 'It is a miracle,' Maria exclaims. 'Hold on', the photographer says, and closes her hand with his, as if that could capture and hold the image. Moments later, the working class woman is on her way out of the shop with a valuable, complicated machine: a camera. She opens and closes her fist, mirroring his movement. She is on her way to capture life.

This scene takes place about half an hour into *Everlasting Moments* (*Maria Larssons eviga ögonblick*) (2009) by Jan Troell, one of Scandinavia's best-known directors. Troell has directed feature films, documentaries, shorts and television series since the 1960s, and has received numerous national and international awards for his work.[1]

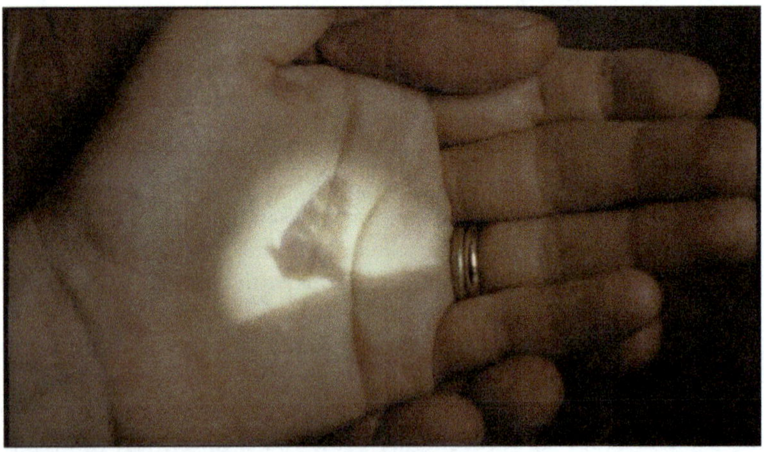

Figure 5.1 Protophotographic image; Maria is learning to capture reality by way of light.

The scene described above explains why the real Maria Larsson, in 1907, took up photography instead of pawning the camera she had won in a lottery, thereby forgoing much needed money for her large family. *Everlasting Moments* is a historical film, partly based on a true story, recounted in Agneta Ulfsäter-Troell's book.

5.1 Based on a true story

The film refers directly to *Att människan levde. Maria Larssons eviga ögonblick* (*Testimony to Life. The Everlasting Moments of Maria Larsson*) (2007), written by Jan Troell's wife, Agneta Ulfsäter-Troell. Ulfsäter-Troell's book is a relatively conventional description of several generations of a Swedish family, offering a miniature version of the background of the modern Swedish welfare state going back to the impoverished and class-divided Sweden of the nineteenth century. Ulfsäter-Troell received much of the information from Maja Öman (her father's cousin), who is Maria Larsson's daughter. However, the relationship between film, book and historical fact is far from clear-cut, not generally, and not in this particular case. The question of 'based on a true story' in film has been discussed by Thomas Leitch, who noted that 'the claim to be based on a true story is always strategic or generic rather than historical or existential' (Leitch 2009: 282). There is a tendency in Troell's filmography to base his films on true stories or historical events: *Il Capitano* (1991), *Hamsun* (1996) and *Dom över död man/Truth and Consequence* (2012) are based on historical figures – and this is true also in the documentaries *En frusen dröm/A Frozen Dream* (1997) and *Närvarande/Being Present* (2003). Even in *Utvandrarna/The Emigrants* (1971) and *Nybyggarna/The New Land* (1972), films based on the novels by Vilhelm Moberg, historical reality forms the background for fiction.

Everlasting Moments deals with the story of Swedish woman Maria Larsson (Maria Heiskanen) who, in the early twentieth century, wins a camera in a lottery, and her subsequent experiences of experimenting with photography. She is married to Sigfrid (Mikael Persbrandt), a charming but often drunk, sometimes violent, working-class man, for whom she bears seven children. Her meeting with the photographer Pedersen (Jesper Christensen) opens her eyes to new perspectives and dimensions in life.

The film conveys two parallel stories: the authentic account of Maria Larsson's turbulent life with her husband in early twentieth-century Sweden, and the story of an unusual woman's fascination with photography. Referred to in this way, the two main dimensions of the film appear: a strongly engaging, relatively straightforward story, and a less direct, but still very important narrative focusing on photography as both an aesthetic and a social alternative to a tough and demanding working-class life.

Reception and background

In international media, the reception was generally positive: *The Guardian*, for instance, hailed it as 'a true masterpiece' (French 2009) and in *Variety* the film received an almost lyrical review:

> Aesthetically, *Everlasting Moments* could scarcely be more at odds with contemporary fashion; in a time when cinematic images are manipulated, degraded or altered, Troell's continued use of mostly natural light seems like a bracing rediscovery of a style that was fairly commonplace, and highly valued, in the '60s and '70s. Beholding Troell's exquisite images is like having your eyes washed, the better to behold moving pictures of uncorrupted purity and clarity. Troell's style has never changed, yet witnessing it again, or for the first time, has the power of a revelation.
>
> (McCarthy 2008)

Although *Everlasting Moments* has been celebrated as an artistic achievement and has received multiple nominations and awards, it was also considered to be somewhat traditional and conventional.[2] For instance, in the Norwegian newspaper *VG* the movie was considered traditional, but in a good way, while *Filmmagasinet* gave a negative review (Selås 2009; Anonymous 2009)

However, the film is far more complex than it initially appears, in particular with regard to media representation, which in this particular case study relates to the question of adaptation. Using an open definition of 'adaptation', it could be argued that *Everlasting Moments* is an adaptation of both a photograph, of a written family chronicle, and even as an 'adaptation' of real life, because the film is explicitly 'based on a true story'. This fits well with the overall tendency in Troell's work to adapt stories from real life, both as fiction films and as documentaries.

Our aim in this analysis, mirroring the general purpose of the book, is to demonstrate how our intermedial approach allows for a productive interpretation of the film. The analysis will enable us to understand the complex relationship between photography and cinema embodied in the film. We will consider the film as an adaptation, but we are more interested in how it works as an adaptation of a photograph, and less interested in the traditional approach from novel (or book) to film.

Discussing the question of novel to film adaptation with regard to Joe Wright's adaptation of Ian McEwan's *Atonement* (2007), Christine Geraghty has observed that an interesting aspect of many adaptations is that they tend to foreground media. According to Geraghty, adaptations:

> often involve a layering of narratives, performances, and/or settings in which one way of telling a story is set against another. Such a layering is often indicated by the foregrounding of media signifiers which invite the audience to set one media experience against another, just as the process

of adaptation involves shifting from one mode of media production to the other.

(Geraghty 2009)

Everlasting Moments, we argue, foregrounds and represents medialities in line with Geraghty's thesis. The film is by turns a relatively straightforward story of love, social needs and the relationships between the generations and the sexes in a historical setting, and a highly sophisticated, if somewhat understated, media-theoretical and media-historical film. This is what we will try to establish in the three steps of our analysis. The first step will be brief because we will spend most of the available space on an elaborated discussion of the liaison between cinema and photography.

Inspired by Geraghty, we will use a slightly modified version of the three-step method. After a brief overview of the presence of medialities, combined with an initial discussion of the function of this rich presence, we will, in the longer and rather theoretically inclined second step of the analysis, investigate in depth the role photography plays in the film, and discuss this in light of ideas about the differences between film and photography. Medium specificity – as defined in the Introduction – will play an important role in the theoretical discussions, and we will analyse in particular a number of other still or semi-still sequences in Troell's film that we find particularly important. In the third step we will frame the internal relationship between cinema and photography.

An even more specific aim of this case study is to include the discussion of stillness, movement, cinema and photography in the analysis of Troell's seemingly straightforward narrative film. *Everlasting Moments* enters this important but complex discussion in its own subtle way, while addressing the status of both cinema and photography in what has been termed our 'post-medium' condition.[3] In so doing, the film raises a number of questions concerning media theory and media ontology. Are the differences between cinema and photography essential, in spite of the similarities between them, and to what degree can the differences be framed within the traditional divide between cinema's motion and photography's stillness? Is photography the 'best' medium with which to capture life or create everlasting moments? Is the film medium better at bringing frozen moments back to life? And what happens when the two medialities meet in *Everlasting Moments*?

Step one: cataloguing media in *Everlasting Moments*

From the very first introductory shot of the film, to its final image, the viewer encounters a range of different media; it could be argued that the film presents a history of visual media. Viewers can follow – in a non-chronological version – a display of visual medialities, from the 'earliest' instance (shadow puppets) to more contemporary visual media, almost impossible to see because it is the very medium 'through' which one sees the representations of the film. Furthermore, the film creates a paragone of the represented medialities, an antagonistic representation of and competition between the borders and functions of media in which photography and cinema, in particular, play the leading antagonistic roles.[4]

Visual media are privileged in the film, as they are in Maria's life. These media (photography and cinema) serve a number of different functions, primarily as a means of achieving freedom: freedom from hard work and harsh reality, freedom as escapism in the movie theatre, and economic freedom, too, because photography becomes a source of income for Maria and her family. In sum, visual media serve as entertainment, to document the present and remember the past (including an important portrait of the deceased child of a neighbour), and as an artistic and creative force in people's lives. For Maria, it is photography that makes all this possible, while for Pedersen it is both photography and cinema, as it also seems to be for director and photographer Troell.

Everlasting Moments transfers many significant features of Agneta Ulfsäter-Troell's book to the film, including the violent and problematic marriage of Maria and Sigfrid (Sigge), the rise from poor beginnings to a more stable household economy, and the raising of several children.

According to the book Maria Larsson did, in fact, win a camera in 1900 and some years later became an enthusiastic photographer. It is also interesting to note that Jan Troell not only adapted a textual source with numerous photos (Ulfsäter-Troell's account), he actually created a 'cinematic ekphrasis', making a film that specifically recapitulates visual material, the actual photos taken by Maria Larsson.[5] An authentic photograph exists of the real Maria Larsson dancing with her husband Sigfrid, taken by their daughter Maja, and a very similar photo is represented, both as moving images and as a still, in the final moments of the film. This authentic photograph must be understood as an image of something that really happened, a direct meeting with something true.

Step two: structuring medialities in *Everlasting Moments*

In the second step of the analysis we will pursue medial relationships in the film, namely between cinema and photography. The relationship between film and photography shares a long and complex history, as shown by David Campany in *Photography and Cinema* (Campany 2008). '[W]ere we to survey all the moments in which cinema deploys photos (and they are countless), we would find most often they concern its complex status as evidence', Campany claims (this is a question that we discuss in relation to *Zero Dark Thirty* in Chapter 7). 'Whether in mainstream or avant-garde, modern or postmodern film, the proof of photography as memory or history is nearly always at stake' (Campany 2008).

This is partly true in *Everlasting Moments* but, more importantly, in this film Troell achieves a cinematic position that goes beyond both the idea of photography as proof and the dichotomy between cinema and photography. Instead, *Eternal Moments* occupies a cinematic position in-between. We argue that the film's particular interpretation regarding the rapport between photography and cinema can be captured by the term 'fleeting still moments' or just 'fleeting stills': the film investigates a possible representation between or beyond the dichotomy of the movement and montage of cinema and the stillness of photography.

In numerous scenes in *Everlasting Moments*, we find an intriguing form of in-betweenness of photography and film, the fleeting stills. Our term relates to moments that, in the flow of the moving images, almost merge or 'stiffen' into photographic stills. The fleeting stills appear both in the opening sequence with the camera and in the closing scenes, when Maria Larsson makes photographic self-portraits. They are also found in several of the scenes that deal with developing photographs and in some of the scenes representing Sigge working at the docks in Malmö. The following section describes in detail some of the more significant examples of this aesthetic practice in *Everlasting Moments*, and also discusses a number of other scenes that negotiate the limits of photography and cinema.

Everlasting Moments portrays the camera as a magical machine, capable of capturing moments that would otherwise pass unnoticed. Photography is not only a medium for showing us the world as we know it, or as it was in the past, but also a medium for showing what cannot be seen with the naked eye – a phenomenon with wide-ranging perspectives that we discuss in the context of documentary films' representation of scientific material in Chapter 8 (on films on ice and climate change), and relating to the question of medialities and surveillance in Chapter 7 (on *Zero Dark Thirty*).

In the opening sequence, the camera is portrayed as a beautiful, almost magically enhanced object, bathed in light, as if posing for its own portrait (Figure 5.2). Yet, these 'cinematic stills' of the camera (The Contessa) come to life through subtle camera movements; a hand adjusting the mechanics, or the sound of the 'clicks' tellingly indicating that we are, in fact, watching a movie. Troell's own camera moves towards the centre, focusing on the lens, and in a dissolve between the camera lens and the sunlight from treetops in the summer breeze, the title *Everlasting Moments* appears.

The voice-over, with Maja narrating, begins, 'The week after my mother met my father, she won a camera'. This starts at the dissolve, continues over the slow motion dance of her parents and closes with her own portrait and the narrative point of departure, in 1907, with Maja waiting for her schoolteacher to visit.

This tension between movement and stillness is a recurring element throughout the film. Among the subtle examples where cinema and photography blur into each other are the scenes from the harbour that

Figure 5.2 Fetishising the predigital camera: the Contessa-camera as main feature in the opening titles.

depict Sigge and his co-workers. These beautifully composed and coloured pictures bear a close resemblance to traditional photographs of workers from the era, and their style and iconography call to mind some of the work of Eugene Smith and Alfred Stieglitz, among others. Such shots are often used in film to establish time and setting, but in this case the experience differs. The connotations of older photographs in combination with the immobility of the camera draw attention to the picture itself, rather than to the actions. Despite the dramatic events that are taking place, these pictures function like pauses, like meditative breaks, or as film without movement. The feel and the look of the film are almost like that of an old photograph.

This is the medial structure we will construe in the film. These fleeting stills interest us as depicted moments of the past incorporated into film; they may, in other words, be considered a form of adaptation from a certain school of documentary photography. As such, they occupy an interesting place in the representational economy of the film, and they have at least two dimensions. First, they play a narrative role by contributing to the characterisation of Sigge. Second, the photographs may be referred to as doubly fake indexes of the past (the past being re-presented *and* non-documentary). These 'historical' pictures are created on the basis of general historical material rather than directly adapted from Ulfsäter-Troell's narrative. The geographical setting, for instance, has been changed, probably to facilitate the incorporation of the political strike of 1909.[6]

All these examples linger between motion and stillness, and they also function as almost nostalgic memories of times past and a world gone by. In addition, the presence of photography in film may add a phenomenological experience to its rhythm and movement. This again makes way for a spectator who reflects on the medium itself. In the following we show how photography is highlighted repeatedly throughout the film, thereby creating what Raymond Bellour termed a 'pensive spectator', able to reflect both on cinema and on photography (Bellour 1987).[7]

Stop bath

The relationship between fixed time and movement is also foregrounded in a different way in *Everlasting Moments*, namely when photographs come to life in the numerous scenes representing the developing process. The developing process plays a role in the film on two levels: it is both an important part of the narrative, and intrinsic to the abstract level of the film and its exploration of fleeting still moments. In other words, there is a distinction between photography (including the developing process) as an activity in Maria's life, and photography as part of the meta-fictive and theoretical dimension of the film.

Taken as a whole, these scenes imply the possibility of a kind of aesthetic liberation for Maria Larsson. Photography, in particular the meticulous and lonely process of developing photos, allows her to establish a 'room of her own' in an otherwise rough and sometimes tumultuous life. In this way, the developing process is coloured by characteristics that are diametrically opposed to those of Maria's busy everyday life: silence, calmness, solitude and deep concentration. This tendency is illustrated in one of the central scenes in the film, in which Sigge silently, and possibly sadly, watches Maria developing her photographs, clearly understanding that he plays no role in this part of her life. On this level, photography and the developing process, as concentrated representations of individualism and the intensity of photographic work, reveal photography as a liberating possibility for Maria, partly because of the unconsummated erotic relationship with Pedersen.

The scenes representing the developing process have another dimension related to a more abstract discussion concerning the rapport between photography and film. Since they foreground the mechanical process and lineage of (analogue) photography, these scenes may be seen as a nostalgic representation of analogue photography and what has been lost in the digital era. Troell seems to imply that what is lost is not merely the more 'direct' indexical relation, but also the creative process, the photographer as magician. The developing process is depicted as a moment of wonder, almost as something ecstatic, for Maria Larsson. It is tempting to read *Everlasting Moments* as a philosophical statement about the possibilities of (analogue) photography: photography can make us see the unseen, catch eternity in the moment and even teach us to cherish the moment. As her photographic mentor and Platonic love interest, Pedersen, claims in the film, Maria has the 'gift of seeing', and in the film this gift is strongly connected to photography. Characteristically, when this gift is turned into a commercial idea, the developing process is depicted in broad daylight, shorn of its mystical undercurrents, in stark contrast to the magical nocturnal developing moments in which time and eternity seem to meet in the primitive dark room in Maria's apartment.

However, the developing scenes have yet another meaning in the film, concerning what is referred to above as the media specificities of film and photography (motion and stillness). Rather than illustrating the function of photography and the developing process per se, the images represent Troell's most concentrated exploration of a middle position between film and photography. Significant in this regard is that Troell establishes the process as both motion *and* stillness. In the representational economy of the film the stillness of the photographs is blurred, moved and slightly distorted (an example of which is provided below) in front of our eyes. In these instances, a mystical moment is represented as the viewer watches the photographs themselves. The transformation from fleeting reality to 'everlasting moments' is clearly a triumph of the indexical, realistic still moment being produced. However, Troell is eager to stress the moving, fluid liquid surface covering these 'moments', a surface that seems to 'move' the still images. This serves as a reminder that a filmic still is also an identical photo repeated 24 times a second. Although Troell may be restrained in his metafictive argumentation, as touched upon above, these scenes – spread out in narratively central positions in the story – have a readily apparent meta-representational dimension. Facing these moving still scenes, the spectator occupies a new viewing position, somewhere between that of viewing photography and cinema. Or rather, the spectator occupies two positions simultaneously. The image in question is still and moving at the same time: it is a fleeting still.

The final scene of the film serves as our last example of its negotiation of the relationship between stillness and movement, photography and cinema. In an elegant sequence, the film manages to recapitulate the two intertwined dimensions of the film, namely the problematic and violent relationship between Sigge and Maria, and the more philosophical relationship between death, memory and photography.

The brief dance scene, with Sigge and Maria engaged in a loving embrace, is repeated as a visual echo of the opening. This time the scene is accompanied by a different part of Maja's narrative on the voice-over, contemplating her parents' relationship ('Maybe it was love' that kept Maria from leaving Sigge) and her mother's relationship with photography: 'When mother looked at her pictures, she used to say: Imagine, here we are, forever. And these moments shall remain here for eternity'. When Maja takes a step forward to capture a moment of happiness between her parents, using her mother's camera, something changes. The motion slows down and the joyful fiddle music is replaced by the melancholic theme used earlier in the film at times of sorrow. Then, in the middle of a turn in which Sigge has caught Maria in the air, the movement comes to a full stop, a freeze frame. The moment is captured *as* a photo, a frame held for five or six seconds as the colours dissolve and the freeze turns into black and white.[8] At this very moment, the film brings a frozen moment back to life by adapting the authentic photo; at the same time, it may be the moment that most truly captures the life of Maria Larsson. The actual photograph of the real Maria Larsson, or indexical evidence, is not present and therefore not known to the uninformed spectator. By way of his subtle cinematic technique and fictive moment of photographing, however, Troell brings back 'what has ceased to be' and adapts a lived life to the screen. In so doing, he makes a subtle meta-comment on his own filmmaking.

As the photo is held frozen (by way of a cinematic illusion, of course), the sound of a ticking clock replaces the music, forming a sound bridge into the image of a butterfly making its way slowly up a window and Maria sitting and looking at her photographs, while Maja says that her mother will die soon. Maria looks at herself in the mirror, grasps her camera and creates her own photographic self-portrait (by way of the mirror). She then takes one look at the butterfly and opens the window to release it. This movement creates an echo of the scene in which Pedersen taught Maria about the wonders of photography with his 'trick' of catching a butterfly in Maria's hands (Figure 5.3, Figure 5.4).

The last image is a cinematic still that shows Maria's self-portrait, her only one, developed after her death (that information is provided by Maja's voice-over). Troell's camera moves away from Maria, holding her frozen gaze, the only movement the waves in the liquids of the red stop bath. The red waves echo the breeze and the light from the trees in beautiful colours that change from yellowish sunbeams through the treetops (mirroring the very first shots of the film) into a deep red. This intense colour may at first be associated with the inner blood red image of closed eyes turned directly toward the sun. The viewer soon recognises the colour as the red developing light slowly disclosing the

Figure 5.3 An original photo of Sigge and Maria . . .

Figure 5.4 . . . represented as a photo in *Everlasting Moments.*

en face self-portrait of Maria. The portrait then fades into a deep black, which marks the traditional ending of the film. The ending thus follows the 'two grand conventions of narrative closure, that allow a story to return to stasis,' according to Mulvey's discussions of stillness and the moving image: the death (of Maria) and the marriage (albeit unhappy) of Maria and Sigge (Mulvey 2006).

However, the film does not close, as one might expect based on cinematic tradition, with a freeze frame, but with a cinematic still, still moving. The closure of the film also focuses not only on a close-up of Maria but, notably, on her photograph in the process of being developed. The fact that her face is shown partly still and partly moving due to the slight waves in the developer strongly underlines the importance of the developing process in the entire film. The film does not, of course, stop; as cinema, it is projected in time, and the moments last, so to speak. But even so, the phenomenological experience of watching the still of Maria is that of a pause, of something passed, of both movement and time frozen.

Step 3: framing the discussion of *Everlasting Moments*

Everlasting Moments enters a comprehensive media discussion concerning the limits and possible essential elements of visual medialities. Medium definitions and the relationship between cinema and photography have moved to the fore of contemporary film and media research as a result of new digital technologies, and new art and media practices, often under the umbrella term of media convergence (see, for instance, Rodowick 2007; Krauss and Broodthaers 2000; Mulvey 2006). Rosalind Krauss's influential post-medium diagnosis (mentioned above) related to film and photography seems to suggest that the two media have been mixed in such a way that film has become photographic and photography has become cinematic (Krauss and Broodthaers 2000). The digital, or post-medium, challenge is twofold and related to the opening questions in this chapter.

First, the film challenges indexicality as the essential trait of both photography and film, since digital simulation can now replace the analogue and mechanical registration of light, thus replacing mechanical recording of reality with virtuality. From this follows, for instance, that the photographs of the real Maria Larsson from 1907 will be considered an indexical sign of her life (see box).

5.2 The index

Since the early twentieth century, historians and theoreticians of photography and film have sought to establish a commonly accepted definition of cinema (see, for an overview, Andrew 2010). One, large group has focused on the cinematic *apparatus* (foremost the camera work and the editing), while another large group favour the more *phenomenological* aspects concerning the perception and experience of cinema. Despite all differences, cinema and photography have traditionally been considered closely related because they share a material, chemical and technological basis, what Bazin referred to as the photographical ontology (Bazin 2009a). In this vein, so-called indexicality has been the premise for several classical theories on photography and film.

Indexicality refers to the physical relationship between the object photographed (or filmed) and the resulting image. The term refers to Charles Sanders Peirce's (1839–1914) theory about sign modalities where he distinguished between icons (grounded in similiarity and resemblance), indexes (based on causal relations) and symbols (related to agreed-upon conventions). Like an icon, the photograph resembles its motif and it can also be read as a symbol for something else. However, it is its indexical quality that has received most attention in theory: the indexical bond has to do with the fact that a photograph of a woman means that this woman has at one point been in front of a camera. Accordingly, the indexicality has also functioned as argument for film and photography's capability to capture reality, or as a truth claim.

Both Roland Barthes and André Bazin stressed the indexical nature of photography and both experienced a somewhat uncanny element in the frozen moment of photography. In his evaluation of photography late in his carreer, however, Barthes stressed that indexicality produces a shock effect, because the subject that is photographed becomes a rendered object, dispossessed of itself, thus becoming 'Death in person'. This again makes us aware of our own inevitable future death (Barthes 1981). In contrast, Bazin considered the indexicality of photography (and cinema) from a realist perspective, as a guarantee of the truthfulness of cinema.

Second, and most important to our discussion, the mixing of media blurs the divide between photography's stillness and cinema's movement. In her book, *Death 24x a Second: Stillness and the Moving Image*, Laura Mulvey states, concerning DVD technology, that:

> [N]ow, cinema's stillness, a projected film's best kept secret, can be easily revealed at the simple touch of a button, carrying with it not only the suggestion of the still frame, but also of the stillness of photography [. . .] the post-cinematic medium has conjured up the pre-cinematic.
>
> (Mulvey 2006)

Just like the fictional Maria Larsson, Barthes beheld the photograph as 'a miracle', particularly because of its ability to connect the observer with the past 'that has been' or 'what has ceased to be' (see, for instance, Barthes 1981). For Barthes – a discussion we also refer to in Chapter 4 (on *Louder Than Bombs*) – these meetings with bygone events can be a full stop that feels like a stab into the viewer, which makes his or her meeting with the historical photograph a naked, pensive moment.

5.3 Movement and stillness

Although both cinema and photography are time-based and spatial, they are separated by their relationship to time and movement. These differences are pinpointed in several of the classical discussions of the ontology of both media. For instance, according to Raymond Bellour, 'on the one hand it [the moving image] spreads in space like a picture; on the other it plunges into time' (Bellour 1975). Susan Sontag, in *On Photography*, elegantly phrases the same idea: 'Photographs may be more memorable than moving images, because they are a neat slice of time, not a flow. Each still photograph is a privileged moment turned into a slim object that one can keep and look at again' (Sontag 1977). For Roland Barthes, photography's relation 'to time' and 'the trace' captured the essence of the medium. In photography he found what he called 'the shadow of the frozen moment' and what he saw was a connection between time, death and photography (Barthes 1981).

While the essence of the photographic is often captured as immobility and the importance of the moment (see box 5.3), the cinematic is related to the opposite: movement and montage. To quote Lev Manovich, 'as testified by its original names (kinetoscope, cinematograph, moving pictures), cinema was understood, from its birth, as the art of motion, the art which finally succeeded in creating a convincing illusion of dynamic reality' (Manovich 1995). Montage, the juxtaposition of images, is considered to be the one thing that is unique to cinema, and both narration and the structuring of time differentiate cinema from photography. Manovich also described the cinematic as a means of seeing the world by 'structuring time, of narrating a story, of linking one experience to the next' (Manovich 2001a).

Movement is also important in Laura Mulvey's definition of cinema and in her distinction between cinema and photography: as she argues, narrative asserts its own temporality; storytelling has a 'here-and-now-ness' to it, whereas photography has a 'then'-feel (Mulvey 2006). Mulvey defines cinema's ability to move in three dimensions: the mechanical forward movement when projected, the illusion of movement and the movement of narrative.

For Mulvey, stillness in cinema is strongly related to photography, and she re-reads Barthes and Bazin in order to gain a deeper understanding of this element. Her discussions suggest that stills in cinema must inevitably be related to our understanding of photography, despite the crucial differences existing between the two media. She points out that a cinematic still may be defined as the projection of repeated, identical photographs, thereby creating the illusion of stillness, whereas photography is not repeated but stands on its own, in its unicity.

Reflections on the nature of the photographic and the cinematic underlie our interpretation of Troell's film from a film-photography perspective. *Everlasting Moments* offers artistic 'answers' to some of the questions related to the post-medium turn. Our thesis is that Troell's film occupies a fragile, but also productive, middle position between cinema and photography. Such a cinematic position consists of a combination of the traditional (indexical) presence-representation of photography and the possibility of temporal narrativity that is often considered essential to cinema.

Conclusion: fleeting still eternity?

A feature of Troell's *Everlasting Moments* is the way in which the traditional plot is counterbalanced by the numerous instances of fleeting still moments and representations of photography. The interplay between the two may be defined as the film's particular cinematic method, whereby Troell is able to balance a psychologically moving theme with an exploration of philosophical and media-theoretical subjects.

In *Everlasting Moments*, Troell probes this issue intensely in the numerous scenes in which photography and cinematic movement seem to be opposed and where death is constantly present. On the one hand, death lingers above the entire film, from beginning to end, simply because it relates to a 'true story' of a human being from a historical past (Maria's story conveyed through Maja's memories of her mother in Agneta Ulfsäter-Troell's book). On the other hand, the very theme of photography seems to manifest the exact opposite conclusion, namely that death can be transcended by the frozen image. This is visually represented in numerous scenes and partly announced verbally, for instance in the voice-over of the final scene, which claims that photography has the ability to create eternal moments and thus confront death and mortality. When opposed in this way, the internal discussion of the film seems to be a transferred version of the theoretical debate on photography as represented by Barthes and Bazin, for example. *Either* images of the past, fictive or real, point to our mortality (Barthes) *or* these images 'embalm' a moment in time (Bazin), rescuing it for eternity. Such an opposition may seem unbridgeable. However, by reconsidering Troell's fleeting stills in the film, including most of the photographic representations, and relating them to some of his earlier works, we glimpse a way out of the unproductive dichotomy.

Troell appears eager to create a certain non-photographic photographic position in *Everlasting Moments*, that is, a position mixing elements of photography and cinema. Our discussion so far seems to have overlooked the crucial fact that the fleeting stills are not stills or freeze frames, but a kind of photography in relatively high motion, or moving pictures at a slow rate. This leads to yet another possibility, namely that Troell's undeniable insistence on the photographic may really be an attempt to recreate 'slowness' and existential 'presence'.

Eivind Røssaak has demonstrated 'how the slow, even the absolutely still, has become a primary artistic strategy in contemporary cinematic practices' (Røssaak 2008). His argument can be roughly summarised as follows: whereas early cinema relied on the almost magically obtained movement for its attraction (Tom Gunning's 'cinema of attraction'), contemporary cinema is fascinated by the possibilities of stopping or slowing down time. Røssaak showed how cinema and video art engage with immobility in order 'to create new attractions ([the Wachowskis'] *The Matrix*), new cinematic excavations ([Ken Jacob's] *Tom Tom*), and new technologies of the self ([Bill Viola's] *The Passions*)' (Røssaak 2008). The question is whether Troell's negotiation between stillness and mobility, photography and cinema relates to these strategies, and what the function of these negotiations then might be. We argue that the film's creation of fleeting still moments, moments *between* movement and stillness, makes him part of an important trend in contemporary visual culture.

Such 'politics of the slow' is a theme that runs throughout Troell's entire oeuvre. In the crucial scene discussed at the beginning of this chapter, Maria is introduced to the magic of photography by Pedersen's ability to grasp the vision of the butterfly and transfer it to her hand through a photographic lens. At the end of the film, and as an echo of this butterfly experience created by the detached lens of a camera, Maria seems perfectly content to simply watch the slow movements of the butterfly, passively observing the beautiful dissolve of the sunbeams through the treetops.

Characteristically, Troell creates the butterfly as part of the plot without preventing the viewer from interpreting it as a symbol of both death and metamorphic revival. In this way, he uses the relative stillness of cinema to show that it can create memorable moments without necessarily, as Sontag claims, coming to a full stop.

As an almost ironic touch, Troell draws attention to medium transformations in the digital age by way of analogue photography and traditional filmmaking, and makes us see the medium itself. Moreover, if digital cinema has two main consequences in relation to how we view film today (new ways of reception and new phenomenological experiences), *Everlasting Moments* makes the latter visible. Perhaps the film's deepest message – existentially, psychologically and media-theoretically – is that a phenomenology of attentive and careful being is a relevant answer to the problem of contemporary human existence, and that such a position may be created in cinema, in fleeting still moments.

Notes

1. Kurt Mälarstedt has offered a relatively detailed consideration of Troell's entire oeuvre, based primarily on interviews with the director (Mälarstedt 2011; see also Dunås 2001).
2. The movie received five Guldbagge awards (the official Swedish film award) out of nine nominations and was nominated for the Golden Globe for the best foreign language movie.
3. A term made famous by art critic Rosalind Krauss in her book *A Voyage on the North Sea: Art in the Age of Post-Medium Condition* (see also Krauss and Broodthaers 2000; Manovich 2001a, 2001b).
4. These representations not only include photography but also the technical aspects of developing photographs and even a kind of prehistory of photography, with connotations of the magic of the Camera Obscura or the Lanterna Magica. Even silent film is present as part of the media-representation in the film. For a useful updated discussion of paragone see Degner and Wolf (2010). It is worth noting that the metafictional aspects related to working with photography, stills and other *Verfremdung*-effects have been a preoccupation for Troell right from the start. Dunås (2001) shows how Troell's first major film, *Here's Your Life*, actively pursues many of the traits that we discuss in *Everlasting Moments*.
5. The term is used slightly different here than in Brinch (2006).
6. See Ulfsäter-Troell (2007). The film has changed the geographical setting from Gothenburg to Malmö, which enables the entry into the film of an important political event in modern Swedish history: the bombing of the strike-breaker ship *Amalthea* in July 1908 (see also Mälarstedt 2011: 357–369).
7. See also Mulvey's discussion of Bellour in Mulvey (2006; 2002).
8. It has been drawn to our attention that this scene is not included in a DVD version distributed in United Kingdom. It is, however, in the Sandrew Metronome Distribution version from 2009, which we have used.

6 Mixing Senses and Media: Epstein and Friedman's *Howl*

Smoke in the air. Sounds of people mumbling. Wine being passed around. Clothes and other details tells us that we are in the US in the fifties. In a venue that looks like a garage with paintings on the walls, an expectant audience waits for the show to begin. In front of them a young man is checking his manuscript, putting on his reading glasses. The sound of a guitar adds to the impression that, perhaps, a rock concert or some other kind of performance is about to happen. The black and white picture adds to the authentic touch of time and setting. The camera moves among the audience as the young man begins his performance, saying 'Howl – to Carl Solomon', while the written words 'San Francisco 1955' appear on the screen. He reads the opening lines from *Howl*:

> I saw the best minds of my generation destroyed by madness, starving
>   hysterical naked,
> dragging themselves through the negro streets at dawn looking for an
>   angry fix,
> angelheaded hipsters burning for the ancient heavenly connection to
>   the starry dynamo in the machinery of night,
> who poverty and tatters and hollow-eyed and high sat up smoking in
>   the supernatural darkness of cold-water flats floating across the tops
>   of cities contemplating jazz,

At the word 'jazz' a non-diegetic jazz tune starts playing, and the image of the poetry reading freezes and shrinks to a fifth of the screen. The split screen is divided into footage of James Franco (this time in colour) re-enacting an interview as Allen Ginsberg; black and white footage of a window exhibition of the book *Howl*; a still photo (in black and white) of a young Allen Ginsberg, and a painting of a young man with glasses (resembling a young Ginsberg). The title sequence continues with split screen images of the City Lights book store in San Francisco, authentic photos of Ginsberg, gay rights demonstrations, newspaper clippings, names of the actors, animations and scenes from the film about to begin, until it ends with an intertitle on a black and white background stating: 'In 1955, an unpublished twenty-nine-year old poet presented his vision of the world as a poem in four parts. He called it . . .' The next scene

Figure 6.1 The title sequence, which mixes archival photos of Allen Ginsberg with new footage of James Marco, juxtaposed with copies of *Howl*.

shows an underpass in black and white, and the title *HOWL* appears as the poet (James Franco) walks through it, perhaps symbolising his transformation from ordinary man to famous author, from nobody to celebrity. Franco stops, looks into the camera and the text continues: 'His name was Allen Ginsberg' (Figure 6.1).

The first part of this complicated opening sequence in Epstein and Friedman's *Howl* (2010) offers a fictive representation of a real historical event: the first performance of the poem *Howl*, read live by Allen Ginsberg at the Six Gallery in San Francisco on 7 October, 1955.[1] Lawrence Ferlinghetti published *Howl* shortly thereafter. Some 520 copies of the London-printed poem were seized by customs officials on 25 March, 1957, and two months later Ferlinghetti was arrested and charged with selling obscene material or, to quote the prosecutor in the resulting trial, 'filthy, vulgar, obscene, and disgusting language'. Thus began the case of *The People v. Ferlinghetti.*

As this description of the film's opening suggests, and as we want to foreground in our reading of *Howl*, the film relies heavily on a rich mixing of different media. Therefore, the immediate aim of this chapter is to discuss the complex medial (but also sensorial) relations in the film *Howl* and in doing so we will be able to demonstrate how perspectives from intermedial theory can be useful when analysing the film. Following our generally proposed method we will, in our first step, primarily catalogue the most important intermedial elements in it. The results of this will then be worked into two structures inherent in the catalogued intermedial material: first, what we call an intersensorial analysis, and secondly a more critical discussion of the two fundamental intermedial aesthetic regimes that collide in this film. These two steps will lead us to the third and final part of the analysis, where we contextualise and discuss our findings.

Our aim in this chapter is, consequently, to illustrate how this intermediality is not only a main characteristic of this particular film, but a formal characteristic that needs to be understood in more general aesthetic terms.

6.1 Allen Ginsberg's *Howl* (1956)

Howl represents a number of named and unnamed persons, famously called the 'best minds of my generation' in the poem's opening words. These people are not the conventional American citizens of the 1950s, but rather drug addicts, poets, musicians, and the mentally ill, described in a style and in settings similar to what Russian literary critic and philosopher Michail Bakhtin in another context called 'slum naturalism' (Bakhtin 1984). These depicted persons, including the omnipresent narrator of the text, engage not only in political exclamations far from the mainstream of their time, but also in explicit sexual relations, both heterosexual and homosexual (which was the main reason behind the 'obscenity trial', conducted at a time when sodomy laws made homosexual acts a crime in all US states).

Formally, the poem exemplifies Ginsberg's attempt to find a lyrical mode that suits his hallucinatory visions as well as his formal needs of structure and ordering. In the years preceding *Howl* he had, according to his own accounts, developed the paratactic structure dominating *Howl:* with the opening repetitive 'Who' (in part 1), 'Moloch' (part II), 'I'm with you in Rockland' (part III), 'Holy' ('Footnote to Howl'). Ginsberg is creating a long-line verse form based on the length of human breath, and his inspiration for these repetitive long-liners comes, again according to himself, from music: 'The line length – you'll notice that they're all built on bop [a form of modern jazz] – you might think of them as built on a bop refrain – chorus after chorus after chorus – the ideal being, say, Lester Young in Kansas City in 1938, blowing 72 choruses of 'The Man I Love' 'til everyone in the hall was out of his head.'[2] The language of the poem is set in a vernacular tone as opposed to a more standardised poetic diction, but this does not prevent it from clearly forming a link in the chain of the great, semi-mystic visionaries of Western poetry: Blake, Rimbaud, Baudelaire, Whitman. The formal experiment, inspired by the bebop improvisations, fits the transgressive political and sexual content of the poem, but the main structuring principle is nevertheless the epiphanic visions expressed by the quasi-divine poet and his voice.

Background and reception

Howl still was a formally and politically charged poem as it approached its 50th Anniversary in 2006, which made the secretary of the estate of Allen Ginsberg (Ginsberg died in 1997 at the age of 70) ask filmmakers Rob Epstein and Jeffrey Friedman to transform the story of the poem and the trial into a documentary. Coming from a documentary tradition, with gay-rights-related productions such as *The Times of Harvey Milk* (1984) and *Celluloid Closet* (1995) behind them, Epstein and Friedman were the obvious choice to direct, but their 'adaptation' of *Howl* transformed into something different from a traditional documentary. During pre-production the filmmakers discovered the artist Eric Drooker through his collaboration with Ginsberg on *Illuminated Poems* (1996), and they decided to include animated versions of his illustrations of *Howl* in the film. The animations were thus integrated with re-enactments of actual incidents related to *Howl*. The dialogue in these enactments are based on interviews with Ginsberg as well as original transcripts from court. In the main part of the film Ginsberg is portrayed by actor James Franco, but he is also portrayed in Drooker's drawings, by way of authentic photographs and in an authentic video of Ginsberg performing a song.

The finished film is mixed in many different senses of the word, for instance in terms of genre: it may be described as a *portrait* of Allen Ginsberg, but it is also a *semi-documentary* about the 1957 obscenity trial against publisher Lawrence Ferlinghetti. The film may also be described as an *adaptation* of a literary text (the poem *Howl*) into the long, animated sequences of the film. The film is part of the popular 'biopic' trend of recent decades, where authors and their work have been the object of feature films. The film is also part of a contemporary tendency to challenge the borders of documentary film via a blurring of the boundary between fiction and documentary.[3]

Like Ginsberg's poem before it, the film *Howl* received a mixed critical response, but for different reasons. Most critics acknowledged the directors' ambition in creating a biopic, a semi-documentary directly relating to a politically charged question of censorship, as well as a psychedelic animated universe to match the vital artistic genius of Ginsberg – in one film. Still, even experienced reviewers such as the *New York Times'* A. O. Scott had difficulties placing such a film inside a conventional genre form, and thus described it as '[n]ot quite a biopic, not really a documentary and only loosely an adaptation' (Scott 2010). The critical response consisted for the most part of evaluative questions concerning fidelity towards the author, the historical epoch or the poem itself, including several very negative evaluations of Drooker's animations.[4]

However, the almost overwhelming mixing of media is seldom touched upon, let alone discussed theoretically or critically – accordingly this is what we will move on to discuss.

Step one: cataloguing medialities in *Howl*

Like most critics, we appreciate the way *Howl* differs from mainstream biopics through layering different media: the media-mixture is salient in both the film representation of the poem *Howl* and the representation of the author Ginsberg, and we want to take a closer look at some of the representations of media in the film as the first step of our analysis. However, because we have, in the earlier chapters, given examples of more conventional ways of representing this list of medialities, we allow ourselves in this chapter to give a more 'relaxed' presentation of the most important medialities in the film.

Like Trier's *Louder Than Bombs*, *Howl* is characterised by numerous jumps back and forth in time, but the flow of the film's non-chronological sequence can be separated into five temporal strata:

- the early life of Ginsberg (including his first poetry reading), restaged in black and white;
- stock film from the 1950s (both political and cultural incidents, as well as what seems to be private recordings);
- the restaged courtroom drama of the obscenity trial in 1957;
- an interview with Ginsberg (like the trial, this is restaged in colour);
- and finally, the animated sequences (following Prince 2012).

The poem in itself plays an integrated role in three of these strata, in the early life block (the reading at Six Gallery), as evidence in the court block and, first and foremost, in the animated sequences where it is represented both aurally (read by Franco) and visually (Drooker's drawings).

Let's begin with the famous beat-poem itself, characterised briefly in box 6.1. In the film the poem is represented through a poetry reading in the opening of the film, but it is also read out loud as evidence in court. Furthermore, we see the poem as written text, but also visually transformed into the animation work of artist Eric Drooker.

The heterogeneity of the opening sequence previously referred to is typical of the style and important for the content of the entire film: it consists of a mixture of old and new footage, still photos (both authentic and restaged), animation film, paintings and different texts, as well as a soundtrack mixing spoken-word poetry and different music genres. During the first seven minutes of the movie, fragments of the poem, for instance, are not only read aloud in two different settings, but are also represented through the animation of Drooker's illustrated version of *Howl*, in a mixture foregrounding both similarities and differences between media.[5] In *Howl* however, this technique is not confined to the opening, but dominates the film to such an extent, we argue, that the mixing of media is central to the entire aesthetic output of the film.

The animated sequences draw the attention towards the medialities even more so because they are combined with more conventional filmmaking such as the restaging of real events in the based-on-a-true-story tradition. A more conventional film-analytical approach (say the method suggested by Bordwell and Thompson (2017), mentioned in our Introduction), would discuss production conditions, narrative, or style (such as cinematography and *mise en scène*). *Howl*, however, due to its foregrounding and mixing of media, necessitates a different methodological approach, and intermedial studies offer productive terms and analytical tools.

As discussed in our Introduction, it is not unproblematic to combine the field of intermediality studies and film studies (Paech 2011; Pethő 2011). A preliminary objection is, of course, that film is, per se, defined by combining several conventionally and historically distinct media: written and oral language, images, scenography, performance, sound and music, in other words cinema is a so-called 'mixed art'. Following this perspective several film scholars have now left behind the idea of any kind of cinematic medium specificity. Noël Carroll being the most prominent representative of this tradition (see Carroll 1996).

However, whereas the normative idea of medium essentialism is rejected, the distinction between film and literature is a recurring theme in criticism, and film scholar and beat culture scholar David Sterritt, for instance, argues that the film medium has never succeeded in capturing the spirit of the beat generation, *Howl* included. However, the animation in the film comes close, according to Sterritt, because it is what he terms 'cinema': 'The animated scenes are pure cinema, having little to do with the official record, but everything to do with the free-flowing spirit of the beat generation, which Ginsberg and 'Howl' synecdochically [where a part stands for a whole] represent' (Sterritt 2011).

In our interpretation, on the other hand, we foreground not how *Howl* might be pure cinema (whatever that could possibly mean), but rather we will demonstrate the great extent to which it is in fact mixed media through and through. But let us return to the three-step methodology.

Step two: structuring medialities in *Howl*

After having established and described the rather dwarfing presence of the many medialitites in the film, we will take a closer look at a specific scene from the first part of the film, in order to move on in our analysis from the mere presence of medialities of step 1 to an active structuring of the medial material in step 2.

Following the opening sequence and a short interlude where Allen Ginsberg (James Franco) reflects on his poem in an interview, the film cuts to a black and white scene depicting the writing process, with the words 'Two years earlier' appearing on the screen. In a conventional establishing shot we see Ginsberg sitting *en face* at his typewriter in his apartment (Figure 6.2), but the shot does more than set the scene: the shot is also a nicely composed and very rich mixed media combination. The establishing shot includes, to begin with, three technical media

Figure 6.2 The writer at work on his typewriter, which at first works only with conventional letters . . .

namely typewriter, the gramophone and the telephone. Qualified media in this scene include a record sleeve signalling the qualified medium of classical music (the attentive spectator is able to see that it is J. S. Bach's *Mass in B Minor*), the record sleeve itself being a combination of images and letters, books in the background and on the table, representing the qualified medium of literature (while at the same time denoting also the technical medium 'printed book'), a pre-modern mask on the wall (bordering between craft and the qualified medium 'sculpture', depending on the context). The result is almost an over-saturation, media-wise, of the shot.

This rich representation of medialities subtly prepares for the next part of the scene, where an extreme close-up shows the typewriter typing single letters; 'I - s - a - w . . .' (Figure 6.3). From the typewriter the camera moves to the eyes of Allen Ginsberg, and in the following cut the photographic images are transformed into an animated version of the extreme close up of the typewriter. Obviously, a medium transformation has taken place, but following Elleström's terminology we can specify this rather blunt statement by noting that the technical medium (for instance the TV-screen where we watch the film) and the qualified medium of cinema (the art form) remain untouched: instead it is the basic medium of moving images which changes from photographic moving images to animated moving images (Elleström 2010a, 2014; see also the Introduction).

What we wish to call the 'animated' typewriter produces not only the predictable letters of the alphabet but even musical notes (Figure 6.4). These, in turn, transform into humanoid figures (Figure 6.5), which,

Figure 6.3 . . . but then turns into an animated machine . . .

Figure 6.4 . . . producing musical notes . . .

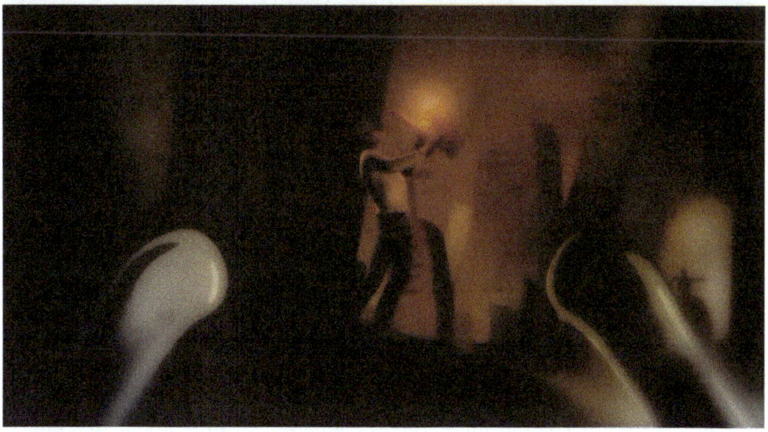

Figure 6.5 . . . and human figures.

in new transformations, morph into naturalistic human portraits. All this in only 30 seconds. This series of micro-transmediations (each of which are made by way of individual cuts; a letter – cut – turns into a note – cut) turns into a human figure. We can conceive of the sequence as one analytical entity in which a number of media or symbols of media (letters, notes, animated figures) coexist in *combination.* However, when including the oral reading of the poem in this analysis, the scene must be described as an *adaptation*, transforming (but also including) the poem *Howl* into the cinematic presentation (see also Chapter 5, on *Everlasting Moments*). These rapid transformations and/or combinations (depending on perspective) continue for the next two minutes, including transformations and cuts between naked human figures, a city, a city transformed into rows of books, fiery abstract figures, and images of musical notes.

But suddenly the sequence ends and a non-animated James Franco as Ginsberg returns momentarily, and the animation is briefly back before this stream of micro-transmediations stabilises into live action film. It is probably no coincidence that on the soundtrack this moment corresponds with one of the more salient sexual elements of the poem:

> who [the angelheaded hipsters] ate fire in paint hotels or drank turpentine
> in Paradise Alley, death, or purgatoried their torsos night after night
> With dreams, with drugs, with waking nightmares, alcohol and cock and endless balls,'
>
> (Ginsberg 1956)

After the opening sequence follows a cut from the extreme close-up of the typewriter (Figure 6.6) to the face of Franco concentrating,

Figure 6.6 An artist's apartment conspicuously filled with artistic objects, such as a typewriter . . .

probably in an effort to imitate the gaze of Ginsberg focusing on the paper where the first words of *Howl* are being typed. The semantic content of the letters also focus on *sight*: 'I saw'. The *sight* of the letters is now accompanied by the *sound* of slow jazzy piano-music and the transformation from photographic images to animated images – also detected by sight – seems to mark the threshold from one regime of media, senses, and reality to another dimension. Or perhaps it is more precise to say that we move from everyday life to a realm of art, fantasy, and borderless freedom where everything is possible, including effortlessly crossing media borders as well as the borders of the senses. The transformation of the letters of the typewriter could now be described as moving from letters (sight) to notes (sight and virtual sound) to human figures.

In general terms we might conclude that the typical intermedial structures of the film *Howl* are process, inventory and *mise en abyme*. But we need to be more precise than that, and it is fitting to state that the even more overarching structural intermedial form, incorporating everything else, is an extreme confidence in the possibilities of the seamless and unhinged transformation and mixing of media. The film expresses a belief in media transformation without any constraints.

However, this description of the structures of intermediality in the film raises new questions, in particular concerning how we can frame and contextualise the relations between media; this will be the subject of the third step of the analysis.

Step three: contextualising the medialities in *Howl*

As explained already in the Introduction, the relationship between media has a long and complex history, and the mixing of media or art forms has been interpreted in two different ways; either in the tradition of medium specificity, tracing its history all the way back to Lessing's treatise on *Laocoön* from the eighteenth century, or in the *ut pictura poesis* (Horace) line of thinking. Medium specificity stresses the necessary and legitimate borders of art forms and media, and '[a]ccording to this line of thinking, any art's essence was to be found in the medium's distinctive possibilities for creating forms or evoking feelings', to quote film scholar David Bordwell (1997). The *ut pictura* tradition, on the other hand, stresses that art ought to transgress media borders, both in order to produce the strongest impression possible on spectators and in order to transgress superficial and artificial media borders.[6]

Framing *Howl* within this age-old discussion can put into perspective some of the formal and ethical questions concerning both the transmediation and the combination dimensions of *Howl*. In the animated typewriter scene discussed above (and this goes, generally, for the film in its entirety), there is absolutely no trace of Lessing's idea of natural medium borders. Instead, the media combinations as well as the micro-transformations produce what it is tempting to call promiscuous media copulations. Without any seeming effort, the film moves between, and mixes, fundamentally different cinematic categories (animation, photographic images and live action film) with subgenres of conventional cinema (fictive court drama and actual interview) and differentiated cinematic aspects feeding into this comprehensive mix, too (intertitles and other texts, music, sound etcetera), and on a even more fundamental level, sense impressions collide in an all-pervasive, proclaimed synaesthesis.

6.2 Digital filmmaking

Digital filmmaking has changed cinema as we know it. Smaller and more flexible cameras have made it easier for cinematographers to shoot, as well as see the results immediately, and almost everyone has tools to edit film on their computers. Filmmaking has become cheaper and more accessible. It has even been argued that *film is dead*, due to the fact that analogue filmmaking (films shot on 16, 35 or 70 mm) is more or less gone. *The Virtual Life of Film* discusses the status of cinema studies in a time when film could disappear, and when such significant change begs the question: 'What is cinema?' However, prominent filmmakers such as Quentin Tarantino, Paul Thomas Anderson and Christopher Nolan have all argued that film is better on celluloid, and Nolan's *Dunkirk* (2017) was shot on film and was screened both in film and digital formats worldwide.

Since digital image processing was developed around 1980, digital solutions have replaced footage in more and more areas. CGI (computer generated images) has made possible a cinematic version of Yann Martell's 'unfilmable' *Life of Pi* (Ang Lee 2012) as well as attractive versions of Tolkien's Middle Earth in *The Lord of the Rings* (Peter Jackson 2001–13) and *The Hobbit* (Peter Jackson 2012–14).

The film *Howl* represents Ginsberg's artistic work and creation in condensed form in the typewriter scene. This scene in particular and the film in general express a highly romantic and gendered idea of artistic creation: the solitary male artist receives (almost divine) inspiration, which he types down immediately, un-hesitatingly on his magical (or should we say *animating*) typewriter. This typewriter produces letters, musical notes, and human iconic figures. In other words: the film shows that the borders of senses and media can and probably should be crossed.

In order to deepen our understanding of the peculiar intermedial argument inherent in the aesthetics of the film, we need to move on to what is undeniably the most conventional part of it, namely the courtroom scenes.

The directors have chosen to place fragments of the famous trial in an almost rhythmic pattern in the overall structure of the film, where the interview sessions and representations of flashbacks from Ginsberg's life alternate with the court scenes, in intervals of ten to fifteen minutes. On the one hand the courtroom theme creates suspense and on the other it frames the flashbacks and the animated sequences in a historical context. Four witnesses are represented in the film, who divide neatly into the prosecutor's and the defence camps, respectively: teacher and former radio host Gail Potter and professor of literature David Kirk stand against professor of literature Mark Schorer and critic Luther Nichols.

The film creates the impression that Potter and Kirk (witnesses for the prosecution) are unable and unwilling to grasp the form and the content of the poem. As an introduction to the scene, Gail Potter – clearly the most satirically depicted person in the trial – is foolhardily sure that she is expressing universal truths about literary art and criticism, when claiming that:

> in order to have literary style you must have form, diction, fluidity, clarity. [. . .]. And in content, every great piece of literature, or anything that can be really classified as literature, is of some moral greatness.

These are, of course, precisely the aspects of literary style she does not find in Ginsberg's text, so, following this pedantic logic, *Howl* does not qualify as a literary work of art. This is supported by professor David Kirk, who claims that a work of literature must possess 'greatness' either in theme or form (as well as being prompted by a suitable 'opportunity'), an intricate set of levels between which, however, Kirk manages to manoeuver without any hesitation or doubt. Since Kirk regards the form of *Howl* to be an imitation of Walt Whitman's *Leaves of Grass*, which was published a century before Ginsberg's work, and *Howl*'s theme to be something as banal as the unhappy life of Carl Solomon, he subsequently deems the work unworthy of the title of 'great literature'. Schorer and Nichols, on the other hand, read *Howl* in its relation to generational post-war desperation, which is expressed in the poem's particular form. Furthermore, they both try to follow its content through the form without establishing one single meaning of the text, and Schorer, consequently, offers somewhat of a textbook definition of poetry when stating 'you can't translate poetry into prose – that's why it is poetry.'[7]

Literary critic Stanley Fish has described the film as a crash course in literary theory, including biographical, psychoanalytical, and reader response readings (Fish 2010). But the courtroom scenes also participate in what we are focusing on in this chapter: the relation between media. Tweaking the borders between law and the arts a little bit, we might say that the prosecutor argues for a position on literature and art that can be compared to that of Lessing and his numerous followers, who advocate that borders between media are natural, morally desirable, as opposed to the supposedly chaotic and morally undesirable, borderless mixing of media. The defence, on the other hand, supports Ginsberg's poem in insisting on bridging and perhaps even destroying the conventional boundaries of literature and obscenity, cursing and non-provocative vocabularies, heterosexuality and homosexuality. When, for example, Ginsberg in the interview sequences refers to a memory of watching art, and clearly expresses himself in a form that is related to the contemporary bebop jazz, it becomes obvious how the defence is also expressing a view that supports the crossing of media boundaries.

Thus we have come full circle and can return to the following question: Are boundaries – between media, sexes, aesthetic forms – desirable or not, according to *Howl*?

Conclusion: between promiscuity and solemnity

It is tempting to answer this question by stating that the film, following the ecstatic and triumphant border crossings of the poem *Howl*, itself should naturally be inclined to follow the anti-*Laocoön* line. That is not quite the case, however, partly because the film (or rather the directors) itself seems to be in doubt. The magical animated typewriter scene, set in an apartment conspicuously filled with artistic objects (Figures 6.7, Figure 6.8), is well suited to staging the triumphant media transformations and producing the ecstatic mixing of media. However, at the other end of the film we find another, much less jubilant version of Ginsberg's room. The final work-place scene (where the soundtrack is identical to the music that opened the animated typewriter scene), occupying the suspense-filled interregnum between defendant's and prosecutor's pleas, does not stress a triumphant, indiscriminate mix of media. Rather, in short but well-articulated cuts, each medium is represented in splendid isolation. First in a seemingly deliberate exhibition of shots displaying isolated qualified media, is the typewriter. The sequence continues with a clip showing a vase with a modernist-style decoration, then an Asian sculpture in the next shot, followed by a photographic reproduction of the Colosseum in Rome, and – in one shot after another – a TV set, a gramophone, and a record sleeve.

The end of the sequence is marked by a semi close-up of Ginsberg (James Franco) lying in a posing position in front of the tape-recorder, indicating that the scene, as opposed to the first intensely energetic typewriter scene, is no longer depicting the creative process. The setting could perhaps even (ironically) suggest a post-coitus state of relaxation?

In the media discussion, which we have argued is an all-important aspect of the film, the two typewriter scenes seem to balance each other out: the creative outburst resulting in the *Gesamtkunstwerk*-utopia of the animated parts stand against the much calmer distinctiveness of the last media-sequence. And it is probably significant that after this scene, the film does not offer any more animated versions of the poem. The final ten minutes of the film focus exclusively on Ginsberg's biography, culminating with a beautiful, moving sequence with authentic footage

Figure 6.7 . . . art work . . .

Figure 6.8 . . . and music.

of Ginsberg himself singing a superb if also very, very simple hymn: he performs his own poem 'Father Death Blues', written in relation to his own father's death.

What conclusion can be reached regarding this complex discussion of media in Epstein and Friedman's *Howl*? Our first hypothesis was that the film reactivates aesthetic ideals that correlate with the romantic idea of the total work of art (*Gesamtkunstwerk*). It is difficult to know whether Epstein and Friedman work with or without the awareness that such ideals may be the object of criticism for being anachronistic and naïve.[8] Thus, instead of simply rejecting the film on the premise that the *Gesamtkunstwerk* is no longer a viable aesthetic strategy, we find support in contemporary contributions to film theory, focusing on the intimate relation between cinema and the senses.

6.3 Cinema and the senses

Within contemporary film studies the role of the viewers' sensual engagement with cinema has become an important issue (Barker 2004; Marks 2000). Intersensorial translation, which is our term for the transformations taking place in *Howl*, may be studied on two different levels: on the diegetic level of representations 'inside' the film, and on the level of the spectators' experience, 'outside' the film. As we do most of the time in this book, we will focus on the first level. Seen as sense representations (perhaps *virtual sense representation* is a more precise term), the setting of the scene, including its significant media-related objects, might be described not only as representing a number of media (as we did above), but also representing several of the conventional senses. The gramophone and the record engage hearing, the sculptured mask engages mostly sight (because it is hanging on the wall) but possibly also touch, the cigarette stimulates (virtual) taste and smell, and so do the cups placed in the room. The present technical media, notably the typewriter and the telephone, engage touch, sight and sound.

Following such an approach we will foreground the way that Ginsberg, in the animated typewriter scene, is writing by *touching* his typewriter, *hearing* the rhythm of jazz and visualising the verbal content of his poem. Viewing Eric Drooker's animated version of the poem while at the same time hearing James Franco's reading of the poem on the soundtrack makes for an interesting example of mixes of the senses and crossing of media borders.

We have tried to show that *Howl* embraces what may be called a *promiscuous* understanding of mixing, both when the mixing refers to media and when it refers to the senses. The directors want to suggest, we believe, that the relation between media as well as that between the senses are examples of unproblematic transgressions. Borders between media and senses may be transgressed in medial products, in other words, and as such the directors indeed enter the long tradition of total works of art.

However, the promiscuous media-aesthetic does not stand uncontested in the film. The much more sober typewriter scene later in the film, representing media one by one, offers a less euphoric version of the impression created by our first meeting with the animated typewriter, and in particular the ensuing animations. In the second typewriter scene a far more restricted understanding of media is subtly hinted at.

Despite our doubts from an intermedial or theoretical point of view concerning the optimistic notion of the promiscuity of medialities, and despite the fact that the film could possibly be criticised for individualising a much more comprehensive and complicated political issue concerning both gay rights and censorship, Epstein and Friedman's *Howl* offers a moving and intelligent version of a major literary text, and of its context, the twentieth century. Furthermore, *Howl* is not only a rare adaptation from poetry (instead of a novel or a play) to film, it also, quite elegantly, includes several aspects that adaptation studies often leave aside when discussing a literary source and the cinematic result: by combining the genres of film adaptation and biopic, the film allows itself to discuss questions of interpretation, literary value, and censorship inside the setting of the film.

The film ends on a serious note of awe and respect towards the personalities that the filmmakers clearly consider the heroes of the story: Jack Kerouac, Neal Cassidy, Lawrence Ferlinghetti, Peter Orlovsky (Ginsberg's life partner) and of course Ginsberg himself. In the last minutes of the film these figures are presented through the combination of authentic photographs and photographs of the actors playing them. And as if this bonding with reality was not enough, the singing voice of Allen Ginsberg, insisting, fragile and intense, fulfils this realistically intended ending. The voice – traditionally a technical medium displaying no distance from the performer (and thus often considered no medium at all) – of Ginsberg seems to close the gaps between fantasy and reality, between an animating typewriter and a mechanical producer of letters. But also between the poem of *Howl* consisting of words, and Drooker's animated version of the poem, which deliberately mixes all the arts and media. The film, consequently, opens an enormous range of impressions, from the promiscuous writer and man Ginsberg – celebrating life, sexually, sensually and medially – on the one side – and the solitary Ginsberg singing a death poem on the other, thus guaranteeing, the film seems to say, the truthfulness of the story. This open relation between promiscuity and solemnity may perhaps be explained contextually by way of the biography of Ginsberg. In any case, it leaves the spectators with the impression that apart from creating a hagiography of Ginsberg and his beat-generation, the directors actively decided not to demonstrate whether they believe in Wagner or Lessing when it comes to the question of mixing media – or not.

Notes

1. On the American DVD version, however, the film opens with a disclaimer reading 'All the words in this film have been pronounced by real persons. In this sense, the film is documentary. In most other senses, it is not.'
2. Allen Ginsberg, 14 February, 1956, preparatory to reading *Howl* at Anna Mann Cottage, quoted at http://web.reed.edu/reed_magazine/winter2008/features/the_beats/4.html (last accessed 30 December 2017).
3. Mentionable in this context are other animated documentaries such as *Persepolis* (Marjani Satprani and Vincent Paronnaud 2007) and *Waltz with Bashir* (Ari Folman 2008).

4. For instance: 'The poem is accompanied by some strictly *de trop* [too much] animation in the manner of those stylised eastern European cartoons satirising social conformity that were once a staple of art-house movie programmes' (French 2011).
5. Prince (2012) offers a close reading of Drooker's graphic novel as compared to the poem and emphasises similarities and differences between text and image (and film).
6. For a discussion of these two interpretations of medial meetings in twentieth-century thought, see Schröter (2010).
7. The two positions (formal boundaries versus freedom of form) may, following the proceedings of the trial, be translated into another conflict. Namely the conflict between a normative understanding of human existence that stands opposed to an openness of morals. The final success of the defence is due to the fact that the judge subordinates the obscenity dimension under the constitutional free speech dimension. Morgan and Peters (2006), offer rich material pertaining to the *Howl* trial, including 'excerpts from the Trial Transcript' and 'From the Decision by Judge Clayton M. Horn'. The full decision, with valuable insight into the argument, can be found at https://archive.org/details/perma_cc_ZQ8M-QVY6 (last accessed 30 December 2017).
8. For a discussion of the history and contemporary forms of the *Gesamtkunstwerk*, see Finger and Follett (2011).

7 Surveilling Media: Kathryn Bigelow's *Zero Dark Thirty*

> For us watching, absorbed in the events unfolding, the off-screen space – what we aren't able to see, what we can't be told – is constantly and evocatively suggested as complementary to, and as important as, what is heard, told, shown.
>
> (Gross 2012)

At Britannica.com, 'cinema' is defined as follows: 'Motion picture, also called film or movie, series of still photographs on film, projected in rapid succession onto a screen by means of light. Because of the optical phenomenon known as persistence of vision, this gives the illusion of actual, smooth, and continuous movement'.[1] Kathryn Bigelow's *Zero Dark Thirty*, from 2012, however, opens with something not usually referred to as 'pictures'; namely white letters on a black background with the words: 'The following motion picture is based on first-hand accounts of actual events.' The text is followed by a totally black screen, accompanied by a soundtrack consisting of a montage of voices.

At first it can be hard to detect what is going on: professional messages going back and forth sound like they are being broadcast over two-way radio (white noise, room echo), mixed with personal messages apparently being delivered over the telephone. Eventually we can decipher the number 93. If the viewer doesn't remember United 93 as the name of one of the hijacked planes that were part of the 9/11 attacks and crashed in Pennsylvania, the text frame 'September 11, 2001' soon acts as a reminder.[2] After this the sound bites escalate in intensity, we can hear 'Twin Towers' being mentioned (first by a news reporter and then by a victim leaving a message on voice mail); we listen to screams, crashing sounds and more telephone calls, including a particularly long, desperate conversation between a woman trapped in the burning building and an emergency services call handler.[3] The last words we hear are: 'Oh my God.' Then silence, followed by a black screen: '2 years later.'

As mentioned in our Introduction, cinema has traditionally been referred to as a visual medium, but this condensed synopsis of the first minute and a half of *Zero Dark Thirty* demonstrates how that notion is a simplification. The elements of the film's beginning may seem straightforward and simple – noise, words, white letters on a black background – but in intermedial terms the opening sequence is quite complex and challenging. First of all, the statement 'based on first-hand accounts of actual events' is an authenticity claim, and a stronger one even than the more common 'based on a true story'. The use of these words indicates that screenwriter Mark Boal and director Kathryn Bigelow have taken a journalistic approach to the events following 9/11, but it can also be said to downplay, or even hide, the role the mediation and fictionalising of the events has. As our discussion will show, the roles that different media play in the film are significant and are directly linked to the authenticity claims in the film. Films based on other material and sources are an important object in intermedial studies, in particular within adaptation studies where, for instance, films based on novels are much discussed (see also our chapters on *Howl* and *Everlasting Moments*; Elliott 2003; Hutcheon 2006; Leitch 2007; Bruhn, Gjelsvik, and Frisvold Hanssen 2013). A film based on authentic material represents an interesting extra dimension in this discussion (Brinch 2013; Leitch 2007). Furthermore, it is almost ironic that this opening is focused on words and voices since – as we will demonstrate – this is so clearly opposed to the rest of the film, which is obsessed with faces and other images as the essential aspect of the process of identification, gathering of clues and production of proof.

Zero Dark Thirty has been praised for its authentic take on the 'true' story about the hunt for Osama bin Laden, but, as we will demonstrate, mediation and particularly the use of screens (as well as off-screen space) in the film are all-important parts of its aesthetics, and in this chapter we will not only discuss the presence and function of medialities, but even probe some of the ethical implications relating to these aesthetic choices.

In this chapter we don't follow our proposed model as closely as we have done in previous chapters. The three-step model of catalogue, structure and context underlies the analysis of this film, but in this case study we have chosen to present the analysis in a less formalised way than in most of the other chapters. We will point to the presence of medialities in several scenes, but instead of isolating this to one step in the presentation, we will mix this registration with discussions of the thematic structures of the film (which are also directly related to medialities). In addition, we want to discuss specific parts of the film in the light of the political and historical context of which this film is so decidedly and explicitly a part.

Therefore, the film will be viewed in the light of the extensive media coverage of the 'war on terror'; as a part of this we will investigate how pictures can be seen as weapons, and we will touch upon the implications of new media technologies that are now used for surveillance (Mirzoeff 2006). As a point of departure for our understanding of this film we follow philosopher Judith Butler's argument that we need to understand that cameras and images are actually part of the fundamentally material aspects of war (Butler 2009). For us, *Zero Dark Thirty* is an important example that demonstrates that cameras and other media technologies are not only communicative tools – they also have a certain, in some cases, ominous agency, and part of the power of medialities is that they participate in deciding how images are framed and consequently orchestrate what we see, what we don't see and what we are not allowed to see (Butler 2009: x–ix). Or, as Anne Friedberg states in the opening of her seminal book *The Virtual Window*: 'We know the world by what we see: through a window, in a frame, on a screen' (Friedberg 2006). We follow her perspective when she claims that, relating to images:

> ... it might be useful to extend Wittgenstein's incisive epigram, 'the limits of my language are the limits of my world,' to its visual corollary: the limits and multiplicities of our frames of vision determine the boundaries and multiplicities of our world.
>
> (Friedberg 2006:7)

Accordingly, the issues of 'in-visibility', 'visibility' and 'witness' will be central to our discussion, and in this case study we will analyse some scenes where these are at stake in more detail.

We will start by giving a short synopsis of the film and some comments on the main topics critics of the film have addressed, followed by an overview of the intermedial structure of the film. Our aim is to show how thematic and ethical debates related to the torture theme gain from a broader discussion of mediation, visibility and surveillance.

A controversial depiction of real events

In *Zero Dark Thirty* we follow CIA agent Maya's (Jessica Chastain) years-long pursuit of Osama bin Laden, from 2003 until he was assassinated on 2 May 2011 in his hideout in Abbottabad, Pakistan. The title of the film refers to the time of the Navy Seals operation, namely half an hour after midnight or 0.30.[4] After the film's opening sequence, the next scene depicts brutal torture. Despite not being part of the same scenes, the initial sound collage functions, essentially, as the justification for a dramatically controversial component in the film. In this first scene, the Al Qaeda-associated prisoner Amman (Reda Kateb) is being tortured by one of the main characters in the film, Dan (Jason Clarke), on a so-called black site.[5] Maya is present as a witness, but she is first introduced as seen from the prisoner's point of view, wearing a mask. The brutal and much debated torture scenes only make up part of the film, where they are a central component during the first half-hour; there is one waterboarding scene later, as well as photographs and video clips of torture and interrogated prisoners. After being exposed to different kinds of torture techniques (waterboarding, sleep deprivation, being kept locked in a small dark box, being beaten and humiliated), Amman breaks down and gives the American agents the name of one of bin Laden's couriers, Abu Akman.[6]

Zero Dark Thirty received a lot of critical acclaim internationally, and several Academy Award nominations (Best Picture, Best Original Screenplay Editing, Lead Performance (Jessica Chastain)); however, it only won an Oscar for Sound Editing. The film also received a lot of criticism, the strongest of which related to what was considered to be the film's take on torture. While several radical critics accused the film of giving a positive view of torture, conservative politicians claimed that the CIA and the Obama administration had leaked confidential information to Hollywood. The filmmakers were accused by the CIA of falsifying historical facts; it claimed, rather, that torture did not play a part in their search for bin Laden (Coll 2013). However, that the CIA and the Bush administration did in fact make use of waterboarding and other inhumane methods between 2002 and 2006, was later thoroughly documented. Director Bigelow responded to the criticism in the following way: 'Those of us who work in the arts know that depiction is not endorsement' (Bigelow 2013).

Among the critics were the radical film director Michael Moore and Marxist philosopher Slavoj Žižek, but they took different positions in the debate. Žižek's view was that the film contributed to making torture seem normal, and that a neutral depiction of torture should be considered immoral. Is it possible to portray the Holocaust or a brutal rape in a neutral way, he asked rhetorically (Žižek 2013). Moore thought people should refuse to partake in a discussion about 'whether torture works', because the real question should be 'is torture wrong'? (Moore 2013). In his opinion the film answered yes to both questions, but since the last question was the important one, *Zero Dark Thirty* would make all its viewers hate torture.

A reason why the torture, however disturbing, comes across as whitewashed is of course that the torture is committed by the 'good guys', and as something they do because they simply must. The torture scenes depicted are far removed from the imagery we know from photographs of real events, such as the scandal of Abu Ghraib (see, for instance, Mirzoeff 2006). Accordingly, one can argue that *Zero Dark Thirty* normalises torture because it is shown as a standard procedure, and that it mystifies the results of torture, because in the film torture works (Corn 2014).

However, the aim of our analysis of *Zero Dark Thirty* is to show that the war on terror is not only fought in torture chambers, but that the media too has become part of the battleground. Because the torture scenes in the film are so brutal, they also cast shadows over the other powers the USA possesses, such as surveillance technology. Accordingly, we want to focus on the role of media technology in the film, and in doing so also cast torture in a different light.

The ever-present media

Because *Zero Dark Thirty* tells such a dramatic story, it is easy to overlook just how important media actually are in the film – and in the reception of the film this dimension has often been overlooked.[7]

Different media are present from the very first scene, in which a CIA agent sits outside the torture chamber and watches everything that happens on the inside on a screen, while at the same time recording it. The first torture scene – despite this important element of mediation and recording – nevertheless comes across as utterly realistic, and it feels like an 'unmediated' and direct event that we are thrown into as witnesses. However, the largest portion of the torture depicted in the film is, in fact, presented to us as photographs or video clips that Maya herself looks at as part of her investigation.

Film critic Manhola Dargis in the *New York Times* touches upon this side of the movie when she, not without irony, notes that 'Ms. Bigelow's last feature [. . .] is a cool, outwardly nonpartisan intelligence procedural – a detective story of sorts – in which a mass murderer is tracked down by people who spend a lot of time staring into computer screens and occasionally working in the field' (Dargis 2012). While Dargis uses this description to show how the film differs from traditional action-packed thrillers, we see this as important not only on a stylistic or narrative level, but also as a central theme in the film. We even argue that the film to a large degree is *about* media, and the relation between media, terror and the so-called war on terror proclaimed by George W. Bush after the 9/11 attacks.

It is through the mediated torture scenes described above that Maya finds the determining clues that lead her to the courier who becomes the key to discovering bin Laden's hiding place. Accordingly, Maya is not a typical protagonist or investigator; instead she is depicted as an intriguing mixture of outgoing agent (in the double sense of the word agent) and passive witness, and this peculiar mix of activity and passivity is an integrated part of her psychological characterisation (and we will return to this later). However, the dialectic between activity and passivity is also, allegorically, a mirror of the role media have played and continue to play in the war on terror in particular and contemporary wars in general. In other words, media are both passive observer and active agent in the film.

Consequently, different media technologies are actually more important than torture in the investigation of the Al-Qaeda suspects in the film, as well as in the final localisation and killing of Osama bin Laden. Technical media, in particular the computer screen, the television screen and the interface of the mobile phone, are present throughout the film. In addition, different versions of photographs (on paper and posters) and video recordings play different roles.

Even without engaging in a more systematic registering of the presence and function of media in this analysis, it is nevertheless possible to note that the computer is by far the most important technical medium in the film. Since their first use outside the torture chamber in the initial scene previously described, computers and computer screens are frequently given screen time. The computer screen is used for watching photos and video recordings of torture victims and of interrogations; it is used for watching news, sending emails and chat messages, and computer screens are of course the main tool for taking advantage of the information produced by surveillance technologies. Computers are present in offices, briefing rooms and even, in a spectacular car chase scene in the film, in a car driving around in Islamabad in Pakistan. Similarly, the mobile telephone is important for communicating both in written and oral form, as well as a channel for American surveillance into the Al-Qaeda network.

Television screens are also important, but in this case, we are more interested in what is shown on these screens than the screen itself as a technical mediality, namely the distinct use of authentic news coverage of the war on terror as well as terror attacks, from different international sources. As for qualified media, it is photography, in addition to television news, that is our main interest. In the following we will discuss the role screens (both computer and television screens), photography and surveillance technologies play in the film, and what this means in a broader perspective relating to contemporary media.

We want to discuss the presence of technical and qualified media related to two different questions: first, we want to pursue the important interplay between on-screen and off-screen presentation in the film; and later on, and as a direct result of the on/off-screen dichotomy, we want to investigate the presence and non-presence of faces in *Zero Dark Thirty*.

On-screen/off-screen

As part of the film's strong authenticity claims, several historical terrorist attacks are depicted in the film, both by way of authentic video clips and documents, and as fictional re-enactments.[8] While the Islamabad Marriott Hotel bombing in September 2008 is integrated into the main plot as something Maya and colleague Jessica (Jennifer Ehle) experience themselves, other terror incidents are reported to them and us by way of authentic imagery on different screens in the film. This is the case with the 7/7 terrorist attacks in London in 2005 (where more than fifty people were killed on a bus and on the London Underground), which are depicted through re-enactments of the events: first we see a series of shots from different areas in London depicting everyday life, then suddenly a tourist bus is seen exploding from a distance. Then we see bystanders filming and taking pictures of the bus wreck. This is followed by a cut to Maya's boss, Joseph Bradley (Kyle Chandler), in Pakistan, watching the news coverage of the attacks both on television and on his computer. The depiction of the attacks in Khobar, Saudi Arabia, in May 2004 is structured in a similar way; first a re-enactment of terrorists entering a building that looks like a hotel, shooting people, followed by a close-up shot of a screen showing authentic news footage from the aftermath (blood on the stairs, and so on), and finally, as a kind of conclusion, we see Maya watching news coverage of this on television.[9] The use of news footage adds to the film's 'aesthetics of authenticity' that Bigelow also established with her 'based on first-hand accounts of actual events' in the opening titles. The use of authentic photographs and video clips invites the spectator to consider the relation between film and reality, and is used to support the idea that the film depicts real events. (See also chapter 8 on climate change documentaries.)

When Joseph Bradley is sent home from Pakistan because his identity as a CIA agent is revealed, we first learn of this via the sound of a news recording while we see Maya driving to the embassy in Islamabad. The next scene shows a group of people inside the embassy building watching, not what we first are led to believe is news on a television screen, but an actual demonstration outside the window. Although Bradley is a fictive character, this incident is based on a real event, when strong voices within the Pakistani public wanted a CIA agent put on trial for the killing of civilians by American drones in Pakistan (Kendall 2015).

Even in the film's version of the hunt for Osama bin Laden, which, thematically and suspense-wise, is at the very heart of the film, watching major events on-screen is a central element. Maya is shown repeatedly watching screens; she is shown watching news coverage of terrorist attacks, and the film is particularly keen on showing her looking at identification photographs of terrorists, and scenes of torture on her computer. In his discussion of the film, expert on war films Robert Burgoyne foregrounds these scenes where Maya repeatedly watches intelligence recorded on DVDs on her computer; she goes back and forth, freezes important images (Figure 7.1): 'Here too the observer becomes the observed, as the character of Maya is scrutinized, held to account by the spectator, by the lead interrogator, and by the victim himself' (Burgoyne 2014).

As pointed out by television scholar Gary R. Edgerton, Maya's position here is mirrored in the protagonist Carrie (Claire Danes) in Showtime's television series *Homeland* (2011–). Both characters are being looked on by us, as well as portrayed as on-lookers themselves (which is related to the dialectics of activity and passivity already mentioned). Edgerton describes their personalities as 'a Rorschach test inviting viewers to project their own selective perceptions' on the female leads (Edgerton 2013). Both protagonists could furthermore be said to serve as two different impersonations of the cultural climate in post-9/11 America: where Maya is determined to solve a clear-cut case, and ends up getting her closure, Carrie, on the other hand, is psychologically unstable, and for good reasons quasi-paranoid because she

Figure 7.1 The observer (Maya) being observed.

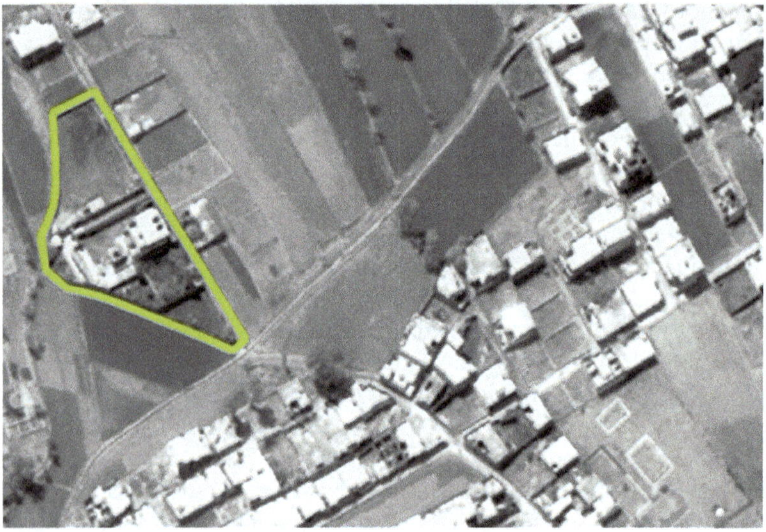

Figure 7.2 Invisible surveillance made visible in *Zero Dark Thirty*: bin Laden's hiding place in Abbottabad.

lives in a world where the difference between good guys and bad guys is getting more and more difficult to ascertain. We have, Edgerton argues, become obsessed with looking and listening, looking and listening *carefully* (to quote the tagline from the American crime series *The Wire*): we are looking for clues at any digital screen near us, as if all of us (or rather all the others) have become spies, because hidden enemies and anonymous terrorists could be anywhere (Figure 7.2) (Edgerton 2013). While governmental surveillance of suspects is, by its nature, invisible, or at least hidden, this surveillance is everywhere present in the film, most notably when the field agents trace the movements of the courier and follow the signals from his cell phone in a car around Islamabad. Here the agents can be said to be able to see him without visual contact, since they are able to follow his movement through their screens.

Accordingly, it makes perfect sense that 'our agent' in *Zero Dark Thirty* is not chasing around in cars or hunting terrorists herself; instead, she is collecting and analysing data that has been collected, either by individuals in the intelligence agencies or by way of impersonal data mining. Most of the time she is listening and watching, and most of the time she is watching screens (see also our discussion of the photograph from the situation room in the White House during the Seal operation below). Contrary to most films that focus strongly on a protagonist, Maya is almost without personal traits, besides her strong determination to capture bin Laden. We get almost no information about her background and her personal life. She is herself a blank screen, which allows for the spectator to project his or her own opinions and emotions on her.

Maya is also surveying the final operation from afar, via screens of course, when Osama bin Laden is finally tracked and killed by United States Special Forces soldiers. However, Maya is not to be understood as a passive spectator in this final phase of the manhunt, not only because we see her role as witness as active and crucially important (she occupies the role as the central witness clarifying the identity of the dead Osama bin Laden – see below), but also because we see the different media as having importance and different agencies within the film's diegesis.

As already argued, *Zero Dark Thirty* is eager to relate the action of the film to historical contexts and facts, and another method for doing this is including authentic video clips of both George W. Bush and Barack Obama. These clips are used primarily as tools for showing the passage of time, and thus the change in administrations during the years of the hunt for bin Laden; but sometimes the video clips have a more specific significance. When Jessica and Maya discuss the possible interrogation of a witness, a clip from an interview with President-elect Obama is running in the background, and the screen is foregrounded as he proclaims the following important statement: 'I've said repeatedly that I intend to close Guantanamo and I will follow through on that. I've said repeatedly that America doesn't torture, and I'm going to make sure that we don't torture.'[10] This relates directly to the 'war on terror', a term first used by George W. Bush in 2001. The war on terror has been an ongoing mediated event since Bush's famous speech the day after 9/11, through the Abu Ghraib scandal (2004) and up until President Obama claimed the global war on terror to be over in 2013. The war on terror has to a large extent been a media war, which in a way was supposed to find closure with Obama's speech: 'We must define our effort not as a boundless 'Global War on Terror,' but rather as a series of persistent, targeted efforts to dismantle specific networks of violent extremists that threaten America,' Obama said back in (2013) (White House 2013). This can be seen as both a political and a strategic change, but it is also a most definite change from visible to more invisible warfare. Since the military intervention in Libya in 2011, causing the fall of Muammar Gadaffi, larger parts of American military operations are performed by drones and, accordingly, American interventions are more hidden.[11] How this strategy has changed, and might continue to change, during the presidency of Donald Trump is of course beyond the scope of this analysis.

Faces and the images of war

The turn towards less visible but still highly deadly and destructive warfare could be said to have started before Obama's declaration of the end of the war on terror.[12] Contrary to the hypermediated terrorist attacks in 2001, the hunt for Osama bin Laden was not a media event (at least prior to the discussions on *Zero Dark Thirty*). So, although the killing of bin Laden is one of the major news stories of modern times, there are actually no official images of the event itself. Neither were any pictures of bin Laden's corpse ever released, despite rumours and fake pictures on the Internet, even though, according to news reports, a photograph of him dead with a gunshot wound to the head exists (see, for instance, Buncombe 2016).

The most famous picture taken of the hunt for bin Laden instead shows the American leaders, including President Obama and Foreign Secretary Hillary Clinton, watching the Seal raid in Pakistan (on a screen, needless to say, which is invisible to the viewers of the photo) while sitting in the White House (Figure 7.3). The picture was taken by White House photographer Pete Souza, and published on social media channel Flickr by the White House. It is considered to be one of the most influential pictures of our time.[13] Although it is a highly dramatic image (if the onlooker knows what is going on), it places the focus not on the violence taking place in Pakistan, instead drawing attention to the politicians (President Obama, Hillary Clinton, Joe Biden) and their security advisors. As such it works very effectively as a propaganda picture, clearly placing the sympathy with the Americans, as well as blurring the actual events. Images of war are important, as are the images that we don't see, and this is also the case within the film. As in *Zero Dark Thirty*, being a witness to these events is made possible by media technologies. In Souza's photograph, we look at agents looking at images (hidden from us) made available for them through the use of drone technology (hidden at the actual scene of the operation). The single most important event in the film, the actual killing of bin Laden, takes place off-screen.

In marked contrast to the non-visualised killing of Osama bin Laden, the mass destruction of 9/11 is one of the most filmed and photographed, viewed, and re-viewed events in history. Consequently, *Zero Dark Thirty* needed no actual images in order to set the viewer's imagination in motion in the peculiarly non-visual opening frames of

Figure 7.3 The hunt for bin Laden followed on screen from the White House.

the film. If we continue our reflections on the black screen opening of the film, we could see it as a critical comment towards the massive visual mediation of war. One point would be that images are not the only way of expressing dread and horror. The sound montage effectively forces itself upon the viewer; it is not possible to turn away from sound, or to close one's ears the way we can protect ourselves from violent imagery, and in that way the non-visual impression might have a stronger effect than the conventional representational strategy. No matter how the opening is interpreted, the 'non-visual' beginning of the film challenges, as mentioned already, the conventional affordances of cinema.

Robert Burgoyne, in a slightly different vein, yet still relating to the medial representation of war, argues that *Zero Dark Thirty* offers a new vocabulary for representations of war. His claim is based on how the film 'juxtapos[es] the spectacle of the punished body with the near invisibility of networks of terror' (Burgoyne 2014). Burgoyne addresses what he calls a 'crisis of violence and visibility': while violence is more visible than ever in the media, victims are becoming less visible. This is particularly the case with the terrorist attack on 9/11. Despite the substantial and spectacular imagery of the falling towers, the attack was also a disembodied event, as Burgoyne claims (Burgoyne 2014).

Illustrative for this point is the photograph of the 'Falling Man' (Figure 7.4). This famous picture of an unknown man falling from the North Tower at World Trade Center during the 9/11 attack was taken by photographer Richard Drew, and although the iconic picture has been replicated widely (in advertising, as part of the title sequence for the television series *Mad Men*, as a theme in Don DeLillo's novel with

Figure 7.4 One rare exception to 9/11 as a disembodied event, Richard Drew's famous picture 'The Falling Man'.

the same name, and reproduced as a series of images in Jonathan Safran Foer's *Extremely Loud & Incredibly Close* (2005), it was also unwanted and highly controversial (Sandberg 2017). The publication of the photograph in *New York Times* on 12 September, 2001 attracted a lot of criticism from readers who found it disturbing, and while it is now on display in the Memorial Museum at Ground Zero in New York City, the museum has chosen to hide it behind a wall with warning signs. Accordingly, the picture has been called the most famous picture no one has seen (Anderson 2011). The image is powerful for many reasons, one of them being the symbolic power of anonymity, echoing the tradition of honouring the Unknown Soldier. Another reason is of course how the change of perspective, from the falling Twin Towers to a falling human body, makes the consequences of the 9/11 attacks more personal.

In a curious reciprocal gesture, it is central to the war on terror that the enemy, to a large extent, remains unknown. The statement from George W. Bush hours after the attack is illustrative here. 'Freedom itself was attacked this morning by a *faceless* coward, and freedom will be defended' [our italics] (Mitchell 2011; Mortensen 2012). This is another way of formulating the quest of *Zero Dark Thirty*: finding and *facing* the enemy is of vital importance throughout the film, and in order to find and identify the terrorists, different media are central, but none more so than photographs.

Figure 7.5 Images of suspects is an intermedial convention in depictions of investigations, images of suspects are often present in *Zero Dark Thirty*.

Zero Dark Thirty follows the convention in crime fiction and thrillers dictating that investigators post pictures of criminals, suspects and witnesses on the walls of their offices. When Maya first arrives in Pakistan, she is introduced to her colleagues in a room with images of suspected terrorists on the wall (Figure 7.5), and during the meeting one of the agents pins a new picture (of Abu Faraj Al-Limi) on the wall below the picture of Osama bin Laden with the comment: 'He is now officially number three.'

Images of faces also play an important part in the interrogations of suspects. A typical interrogation scene will play out like this: we see Maya watching an interrogation or a torture scene (or a combination of the two) on her computer; the perspective will change between a medium shot of Maya by her computer (Figure 7.6), a close-up of Maya's face (Figure 7.7) and the interrogation playing on her screen; during the scene, she will change discs or freeze-frame the video; sometimes we will see different versions of the same interview – the interviews will, however, play out the same way: the interrogator will present a photograph to the suspect and ask him if he can identify the man in the picture.

Through these repetitions, it becomes clear that in order to find their main suspect – Abu Akman – the agents place their trust in photography's ability to provide the secure identification of a suspect. Accordingly, the film follows a tradition established in the mid-nineteenth century, when photography became the preferred tool for identification of criminals.[14] However, their search is in vain and many of their informants claim that the man in the picture is dead. In the end, it turns out that their lack of success is due to the fact that they had used the wrong image, namely the picture of the suspect's brother, who was indeed dead.

The importance of identity and identification, so strongly related to facial recognition, is also important in the last part of the film, and

Figure 7.6 The importance of screens in *Zero Dark Thirty*: Maya by her computer.

Figure 7.7 The importance of screens in *Zero Dark Thirty*: close-up of Maya looking at her screen.

during the final operation it is vital that the person they believe to be hiding in a secure house in Abbottabad *is* in fact bin Laden, who, in spite of heavy surveillance, they have never been able to catch either on video or on camera. Interestingly enough his identity is given twice, first by a soldier at the scene and then later, in the final scene of the film, when Maya identifies his body back at the camp. When the soldier is asked to give a positive identification, Osama bin Laden's body is shown, but not his face. In fact, neither his face nor his image is ever made visible for us in the film.

As the film's closure demonstrates, the difference between seeing or not seeing, visible and invisible, watching from afar and up close, is foregrounded. When the chase for bin Laden is finally concluded, the film also ends, but the closing scene is in several ways typical for *Zero Dark Thirty*. The film concludes with a close-up of Maya's face, fully visible to us. Tears are running down her face, but her face still remains enigmatic and open to interpretation. Not even in this concluding image are we allowed inside her head, and whether she is crying because she is happy, sad, satisfied or disappointed remains an open question.

Conclusion

In this chapter, we have not followed our proposed three-step analytical model. First of all, this has to do with the film in question: *Zero Dark Thirty* is a film that we wanted to discuss within a broader perspective of contemporary media, media technology and war on terror. Accordingly, our primary interest here has been to see how an important issue of our time, the mediation of terror, is represented in film generally and in this film specifically. Secondly, we wanted to demonstrate that a general intermedial perspective can influence a film analysis even when the structuring of the reading differs from the three-step model. Thus we do hope that our inspiration from intermedial perspectives is nevertheless clearly visible in this chapter, and that it demonstrates that our approach can be carried out differently depending on the material or the researcher's own choice. Our investigating procedure has been the same as in the previous chapters: we have catalogued, structured and contextualised media presence in *Zero Dark Thirty*, although we have presented our findings in another way.

Our analysis has shown, we argue, the strong presence of media in the film. In addition, the media presence in the film could be said to be reflecting the role media has played in the war on terror. We have demonstrated that media and media technology play an important role in terms of what is (or becomes) visible – or remains invisible. As Nicholas Mirzoeff has argued in relation to the Abu Ghraib scandal in 2005, the photographs that emerged documenting the American soldiers' torture of the Iraqi prisoners showed us that 'the image, or better, the visual event, in global visual culture is not so easily unmasked, its mere visibility accounting for relatively little' (Mirzoeff 2006). While ethics was central in the discussion surrounding the film's depiction of torture, we argue that ethical perspectives could also be broadened to include the mediation of terror and the war on terror more generally.

We see *Zero Dark Thirty* as a reflection of the dichotomy between the immoderate visibility of terror, for instance through an extreme media coverage of every terror incident, and the questionable invisibility of the fight against terror, for instance through increased governmental surveillance, both of which have large, yet also largely unknown and unresearched consequences for our modern societies.

Notes

1. Motion Picture | Britannica.com
2. *United 93* is also the title of Paul Greengrass's 2006 film about the event.
3. The filmmakers' use of authentic telephone calls from the victims of 9/11 without the knowledge of the victims' next of kin has been criticised.
4. This is how Kathryn Bigelow uses the term, according to Air Force 101 it refers to the time between 00:01h and 05.59h, also referred to as 'oh-dark-thirty'.
5. Since 9/11 the CIA have operated hidden and secret facilities where they detained and interrogated high-level Al Qaeda suspects.
6. Abu Ahmed al-Kuwaiti was the name of the actual courier, and he was killed during the American operation in Abbottabad.
7. An important exception is Robert Burgoyne's article 'The Violated Body: Affective Experience and Somatic Intensity in Zero Dark Thirty' (2014) in which this perspective is included, and that we draw on in our discussion. See also Gross (2012).
8. Re-enactments are sometimes used in documentary film when authentic footage is not available. See for instance Staiger about how this can be seen as a 'trace of the real' (2000).
9. It is difficult to see where this footage is from, and the source is not credited. Accordingly, it is hard to tell whether this is from the actual attack, in spite of the Arabic script on the footage.
10. The news clip used in the film can be seen here: https://www.youtube.com/watch?v=UQXZoM__vU0 (last accessed 30 December 2017).
11. See for instance CBS *60 Minutes II: Inside Abu Ghraib* 2004. The use of drones in the war on terror is a topic in its own right, and other movies engage this question more in detail, see, for instance, *Eye in the Sky* (Gavin Hood 2015) or the documentary *Drone* (Tonje Schei 2014.)
12. We term this a declaration since Donald Trump, while he was running for president, said that he wanted to strengthen the war on terror.
13. See for instance http://people.com/politics/trump-obama-situation-room-photos-compared (last accessed 30 December 2017).
14. See for instance Allan Sekula (1986) on the use of historical photography, and the relationship between photography and physiognomy.

8 Cinematic Representations of a 'Super Wicked Problem': Climate Change in Documentary Film (*Ice and the Sky and Chasing Ice*)

In this chapter we want to focus on documentaries the same perspectives we have thus far used on fiction films. Even though *Zero Dark Thirty* and *Howl* in particular use non-fictive elements to a certain extent we have yet to discuss non-fiction elements in more detail.

We base our discussion on two documentaries that deal with the important and challenging topic of climate change: Jeff Orlowski's *Chasing Ice* (2012), and Luc Jacquet's *Ice and the Sky* (*La Glace et le Ciel* 2015). The first follows the efforts of the American photographer James Balog and the second the work of the French glaciologist Claude Lorius. Both films depict the disappearance of ice as a consequence of global warming, and they do it by relating the thematic of ice to an individual human-interest story. It is our hope that our intermedial analysis of these two 'ice-focused' documentaries will have bearings on both the field of climate-related documentaries in particular, but also other documentaries in general, onto which our analytical points will likely also apply.

In this chapter we will leave aside the question of what potential the documentary has to faithfully and productively represent the complicated problem of climate change. Other researchers have investigated this, and while we certainly believe that documentary has the potential to depict crucial aspects of climate change and consequently to influence audiences in political questions,[1] our main question is rather *how*, in intermedial terms, the documentaries that we discuss are able to do that. As a consequence of our analysis we hope to stimulate interest in more formalistic investigations regarding the ways in which intermedial notions can describe the workings of documentary as a cinematic subgenre. In this chapter we will not use the methodological three-step model, but instead work through our questions in more general, intermedial terms and, as opposed to most of the other analyses in this book, we shall focus less on the represented medialities and more on the representing medialities of the two documentaries about climate change.

We will begin by briefly touching upon documentary film's abilities to represent climate change and then move on to specify our discussion by way of focusing on the intermedial dimensions of the two chosen documentaries, which is the main target of this chapter. It is beyond the scope of this section to provide a detailed discussion of the definitions or characteristics of documentary.

8.1 Documentary

A common insight within documentary studies is that documentary can be described through a special relationship between the film and its subject. Nestor John Grierson, who famously coined the term 'documentary', described it as 'the creative treatment of actuality' (Renov 1993). John Corner has claimed that documentary can be distinguished from fiction by its 'portrayal of the recorded sounds and images of actuality' (Corner 1995: 3), while Bill Nichols articulates something similar by describing documentary as representing the 'historical world' or 'historical reality', thus avoiding the claim that non-fiction film should be able to represent an unmediated reality (Nichols 1991). Nichols goes on to distinguish documentary from fiction not by its form, but because of its content and subject matter: that is to say, the purpose of the film, which has been criticised by Stella Bruzzi (Bruzzi 2005). Brian Wilson offers a broad overview of contemporary as well as classical ideas in the field of documentary (Winston 2013). Among the preferred subject matters in the history of non-fiction film are nature, travel and science, as is the case with the two films in question here.

Climate change

Climate change, arguably the most pressing global problem at present and for many years to come, it has entered policy debate and security management discussions (for general, if also very personal introductions, see Scranton (2015), Ghosh (2016)). Climate change is not only a big problem in terms of physical scale and human impact around the globe, it is also a problem that is both hard to conceive and, consequently, hard to find direct solutions to. Philosopher and literary scholar Timothy Morton characterises global warming as a 'wicked problem': one 'you can rationally diagnose but to which there is no feasible rational solution.' He goes even further and claims that 'as a matter of fact, global warming is a "super wicked problem" [. . .] for which time is running out, for which there is no central authority; those seeking the solution are also creating it, and policies discount the future irrationally' (Ghosh 2016; Morton 2016).

Despite the widespread political and popular denial of the facts, climate change and global warming are well-established paradigms within climatology and its neighbouring scientific fields, and we will not challenge this widespread scientific agreement,[2] but in the following we are not forgetting Bruno Latour's basic notion that scientific discourse is a construction worthy of scientific scrutiny in itself (Latour 1999). More specifically, we will begin by suggesting ways the critical science studies of Latour and other scholars may in fact be partly reformulated into intermedial terms; science, and the representation of science on film, including documentaries, is a question of mediation.

Although climate, weather, and natural disasters play a prominent role in contemporary fiction films – in particular in so-called 'cli-fi' movies, from *The Day After Tomorrow* (Roland Emmerich 2004) to *Snowpiercer* (Bong Jon-hoo 2013) to *Interstellar* (Christopher Nolan 2015) – documentary holds a special position in so-called 'eco-media studies', which is now, after a late start, an emerging cross-disciplinary field combining perspectives from media studies, films studies, activism and science (see, for instance, Narine 2015; McDonald 2004; Stephen Rust, Salma Monani and Sean Cubitt 2013). A landmark here is Al Gore and David Guggenheim's *An Inconvenient Truth* (2006), the Oscar-winning documentary that stirred a lot of attention and discussion about environmental issues. Film scholar Charles Musser expresses the generally accepted notion that documentary film has the ability to sculpt a sense of the revelation of the truth in the viewer, a creation of 'truth value' (Musser 2015). Historically, eco-films have looked at the harm humans have inflicted upon nature, but now the tendency has been that filmmakers shift from pollution and nuclear dangers to climate change. Many of these films have focused on the untold, often invisible, but forceful damage that humans have caused, what Rob Nixon termed the 'slow violence' effects of climate change that hits poor people particularly hard around the world (Nixon 2011). Other commentators discuss environmental disasters, present or future, in terms of 'trauma' (Narine 2015) and thus theorise science fiction disaster films, for instance, as a kind of psychological preparation for future traumas (Kaplan 2015).

As mentioned already, the debate around potential truth claims in documentary has traditionally been interested in questions of visuality, and this has been important in the discussions surrounding the possibilities of representing climate change. A short peek into the discourse may give an impression both of the fascinating discussions going on in the field, in addition to – and this is the point we want to make here – the tendency to focus excessively on visibility and thus a belief in a strong relationship between visibility and truth claims. The attention on visualising climate change has lead anthropologist Peter Rudiak-Gould to categorise three different visual strategies: 'the invisibilists', 'the visibilists', and 'constructive visibilists' (Rudiak-Gould 2013; Hulme 2015). Whereas the 'visibilists' want to see flooding, storms or ice melting 'with their own eyes' in order to believe it, and tend to use what they have seen as arguments and evidence, the 'invisibilists' would rather put their trust in scientists. The people at the frontline of climate change, indigenous people and activists in areas currently battling flooding, tend to belong to the first group. The invisibilists, among them many scientists, hold that because climate change is a complex, abstract and on-going process, it can't be seen – or, to quote Rudiak-Gould, climate change is 'too big, too slow, too uneven' for people to see it themselves (Rudiak-Gould 2013: 123). Rudiak-Gould describes constructive visibility as an attractive middle level position, 'at least on the surface for its compromise between an anti-intellectual visibilism and an elitist, undemocratic invisibilism' (Rudiak-Gould 2013: 123). The third position accordingly can be summed up as: 'Climate change is neither inherently invisible nor inherently visible; it is, like all other objects, made visible' (Hulme 2015).

An important point for us when we discuss the prospect of making climate change 'visible' is that the notion of visibility is either understood metaphorically (visible equals 'understandable', 'perceptible' or even 'true') or perhaps even set aside as a much too narrow concept. We will, as previously mentioned, see the representation of climate change in documentary as a process involving more than imagery in a strict visual sense of the word. In other words, to make something 'visible' in a film, the filmmaker can use all cinematic elements at his or her disposal – and that is actually what the filmmakers under discussion here are doing. But first a few words on the theme of the two documentaries we will discuss.

Why ice?

From cinema to art and literature, and throughout mainstream mass media, representations and discussions of ice, and in particular glaciers, have become popular as part of narrative strategies regarding anthropogenic climate change (Jackson 2015). Pictures of polar bears on melting icebergs have become icons of climate change, but countless other examples exist. In 2014, to coincide with the release of the UN Intergovernmental Panel on Climate Change's Fifth Assessment Report, Danish artists Olafur Eliasson and Minik Rosing transported twelve blocks of ice, weighing a total of 100 tonnes, from a glacier in Greenland and placed them to melt in the city centre of Copenhagen. The pair repeated the installation in Paris, one year later (Weber et al. 2014). As one study put it, glaciers have achieved 'celebrity status' and were even discussed in and featured on the front cover of *Vanity Fair*'s 'Green Issues' of 2006 and 2007 respectively (Carey 2007).

But what are the features unique to ice that make it such a popular tool for representational and narrative purposes? To begin with, ice in the form of glaciers, from a scientific perspective, is seen as a high-confidence indicator of climate change; fluctuations in glacial mass, area, volume and length represent changes in the planet's energy balance (Bojinski et al. 2014). Observations show that the rate of global glacier decline began to rapidly accelerate from the mid 1980s onwards, reaching unprecedented levels during the twenty-first century

(Zemp et al. 2015). Furthermore, ice core measurements taken from Greenland, Antarctica, and high-altitude glaciers, also in the 1980s, provided arguably some of the most definitive early evidence for human-created climate change, and proved vital in shaping the early scientific consensus (see, for instance, Dansgaard et al. 1982; Lorius et al. 1985; Petit et al. 1999). As mentioned already, most indicators of climate change can neither be easily observed by the human eye nor by the other senses (Orlove 2004). We cannot see, hear or readily smell or taste carbon dioxide accumulating in our atmosphere, and sea levels rise on such protracted time scales that changes progress unnoticed. As a result, these parameters are often presented in graphs and tables. Shrinking glaciers, however, are one of the most tangible representations of climate change, which is probably why they occupy such a prominent role in climate change representations. As James Balog argues in *Chasing Ice*, 'the public doesn't want to hear more about statistical studies, more computer models, more projections. What they need is a believable, understandable piece of visual evidence. Something that grabs them in the gut.' However, he neglects to say that in order to grab people in the gut, images, still or moving, are seldom enough, and this will be our intermedial point of departure for our analysis of the two ice films.

Ice and the sky: through Claude Lorius's looking glass

Ice and the Sky (*La Glace et le Ciel*) is a 2015 documentary by French director Luc Jacquet, who became internationally famous with his Oscar winning success *March of the Penguins* (2005). That earlier film depicted the harsh nature of the breeding rituals of the emperor penguin in the Antarctic. *March of the Penguins* became the most successful eco-film to date.[3] In *Ice and the Sky*, Jacquet returns to the Antarctic to portray the life of Claude Lorius, a pioneer in glaciology and climatology. In our analysis we will look at how both the scientist and science are presented, and what intermedial means Jacquet uses to address climate change. The visual dimension is crucial, but it is definitely not the only medial dimension of the film.

8.2 Claude Lorius

Lorius (born 1932) has spent decades researching ice, and forged the ground-breaking idea that air bubbles trapped in the ice may disclose the composition of gases in earlier atmospheres, also developing a method for determining historical climate through isotopic analysis.[4] Research conducted under his leadership demonstrated that the climate during the Holocene (the approximately 12,000 year period prior to our current so-called Anthropocene epoch) had been relatively stable up until recent decades, when sudden and drastic changes have taken place. Lorius' research has also helped demonstrate the important relationship between atmospheric greenhouse gases and the climate, making him an early harbinger of the consequences of the impact of humans on the Earth's systems.

The film follows Lorius' career chronologically, beginning in the 1950s, and is as much a portrait of a scientist as it is a documentary about ice and the sky, and the relations between the two.

The film was shown at the 2015 Cannes film festival to good, although not rave reviews. The review in the magazine *Little White Lies* positively notes that 'the film accrues its power from not bombarding the viewer with statistic-backed doomsaying. This is not a film which uses statistics to back up a hysterical climate change polemic, but a document of the painstaking task that was undertaken to actually discover these chilling statistics in the first place. (Jenkins 2015). The French reception was mixed, and an excerpt from *Libération* sets the tone: 'On the level of form, the film is disappointing. A rather pompous musical soundtrack. A sometimes wheezy as well as redundant text – "Science allows me to see the future." A talkative first person voice-over that is supposed to represent the words of Claude Lorius (spoken by the actor Michel Papineschi)' (Hanne 2015).

The film opens with an almost abstract-looking bluish image that turns out to be blue ice, with a shadow of an unclear shape moving across its surface. Soon it is revealed that that shadow is a man walking over the ice. After the title, *La Glace et le Ciel*, we follow the man as he strokes the shimmering ice with his naked hand, whilst walking into a large blue tunnel in the glacier.

Accordingly, the first impressions of the film are poetic, almost abstract images creating a sense of curiosity and awe. As the man moves deeper into the ice he is introduced as Claude Lorius, through a mix of authentic audio presentations taken from different events he has participated in; the complex medial constellation is replaced with a French actor's voice-over giving voice to Lorius. Through images where the scientist is shown walking in different landscapes, his perspective and aims are presented, with the escalating voice-over ending in intensively dramatic statements. First: 'I have seen how Man, in the space of a lifetime, by burning oil, wood and coal is changing the Earth's climate [. . .] Polar ice caps and glaciers melting [. . .] Islands submerged by water, burning forests, redirected sea currents, storms, more of them, more violent'. After this the camera closes in on the old man's face, and he continues: 'Science allows me to see the future. I'm going to tell you what I have seen. I'm going to tell you my story'. During the first ten minutes the film has established the rhetorical position from which *Ice and the Sky* will show us what we ourselves are not able to see. The case, which has to be proven to the audience, is that climate change is a scientific fact, and Lorius serves as both personally affected eyewitness and distanced expert witness in the case; one that feels and one that analyses and works scientifically. It is obviously the aim of the film to conflate the two witnessing positions into one, but this is not unproblematic, as our analysis focused on media will try to demonstrate.

The semi-religious discourse – Lorius as the *seer*, perhaps in the radical tradition of French poet Arthur Rimbaud (1854–91) – needs support from non-visual media in order to function.

The film goes to great lengths in order to produce a medial transformation from scientific discourse to documentary cinematic style, and it dwells in particular on the methods used in glaciology. The narrative about science is told as a transition back in time, introduced with Lorius looking at the same images as we do: archive footage from his first scientific endeavours in the Antarctic in 1956, when the Anthropocene period began, according to the voice-over. Overcoming the 'inhuman' challenges enabled Lorius and his colleagues to study ice that was formed 400,000 years ago.

Figure 8.1 Climate change is made visible through the eyes, the efforts and the research of Claude Lorius.

The efforts of the research process and the importance of the results focus on visual inputs: it is, so to speak, told through the eyes, the binoculars, and the microscope of Lorius (Figure 8.1). *We* can know this because Lorius has *seen* the history of the ice crystals in his microscope. This pedagogical depiction of research is combined with the display of the sublime beauty of nature, in particular the beauty to be found in ice and snow. The new footage added by director Jacquet is a mixture of microscopic imagery of snow crystals and drone shots of wastelands of cold landscapes, where humans become microscopic.

Situated knowledge – and hidden positions

From a medialities point of view it is worth noting that Jacquet's film is a typical documentary in the way it highlights the referential, realistic depiction of our historical world – and in doing so it tends to downgrade the ways in which the film in itself is a result of a crafted, manufactured, mediated effort. The entire film is basically about enabling the mechanical reproduction of hitherto unseen aspects of life: the visual results justify why we see all the hardships of travelling under inhuman conditions, painstakingly measuring and noting, constructing elaborate machines, and living and sleeping together under basic conditions.

However, the film is rather reluctant to inform the spectators of the provenance of the visual proof of these endeavours. Who filmed all the dramatic action – from what position, and with what purpose? By the 1950s it was probably clear to participating researchers that the scientific expeditions were sufficiently interesting to be filmed (as was the case with the Norwegian Kon-Tiki expedition), and furthermore that the material was to be kept for decades until finally being collected in a documentary like this. In the credits, we are given the information that different members of the polar expeditions have contributed material to the film. This aspect of the film, relevant to many other films of the genre, makes the spectators if not forget then at least not think too much about the fabricated nature of the entire documentary: the efforts to represent the scientific material are set aside by putting immense weight on the results of the scientific work. We might say that the film offers valuable insights into the knowledge production of glaciology, while making the documentary's medial rhetoric more or less invisible.

Comparable aspects come to the fore if we consider Jacquet's documentary in terms of plot. In the case of *Ice and the Sky*, the film is actually following a form that is not so much based in documentary as in fiction, namely the *Bildungs* plot (comparable but not identical to the *Künstlerroman* discussed in relation to Trier's work): the film is basically about a young and inexperienced man growing to maturity and consequently receiving important insights he wants to share with other people. There are different ways to categorise documentary discourse or cinematic form, one of which could be related to the function the documentaries are planned to serve. Documentary scholar Michael Renov, for instance, has proposed four different poetics, or voices: 1) to record, reveal, preserve; 2) to persuade and promote; 3) to analyse and interrogate; 4) to express (Renov 1993). But despite Grierson's early definition that documentary is 'creative treatment of actuality', within some traditions narration has been treated with suspicion (Renov 1993). Film scholar Bjørn Sørenssen claims that the dilemma for contemporary documentary filmmakers is to choose between 'being rhetorical' or 'telling a story' (Sørenssen 2001). We will return to this dilemma as it is at the core of the two documentaries that we discuss here.

When looking for the signs that the documentary is not necessarily 'real' or realistic, other things become clear too, for instance the soundtrack. We must suppose that almost all sound effects have been added to several of the scenes where early and primitive film recordings are used. The musical soundtrack also adds significantly to the meaning of the production: this includes the Russian-sounding orchestral music employed in some of the parts dealing with the cooperation between American, French and Russian scientists. Even in one of the early scenes, the use of sound is important, and sound is sneaked in to add to some of the meanings of the visual aspects. At the beginning of the film, the general musical style of the soundtrack (late Romantic, typical 'Hollywood' style) suddenly changes into the use of actual sounds, and with a Modernist, dissonant musical sound at the moment when the voice-over comments on the human race's destructive and murderous ('meurtrier') influence on the planet.[5]

The film ends with the image of Lorius standing in the middle of the ice (Figure 8.2) raising the question: 'Now that you know too, what are you going to do about it?' The main idea put forward in the film is the call for action, but the film makes its point by way of a strong emphasis on looking and touching, as well as how the gaze of the scientist can make visible to us what we don't yet see – but also by hiding the eye and the cameras and the media that made us see this. Strategically, by way of focusing on Lorius, the film provides a human face to science, in itself a necessary and valuable addition to the discourse on climate change, in which climate change deniers have provided harsh criticism

Figure 8.2 Claude Lorius depicted as a small man facing a big challenge.

of scientists. But from a media theoretical point of view, the film demonstrates the banal but important point that 'seeing' seeing itself is impossible, and that *Ice and the Sky* does nothing to convey this.[6]

Chasing Ice: through James Balog's camera

In *Chasing Ice*, filmmaker Jeff Orlowski's award-winning debut documentary film, we follow American photographer James Balog's attempts to provide 'tangible, visual evidence of the immediacy of climate change itself' as he formulates it in the film. The film follows a project set up by Balog called the 'Extreme Ice Survey' (EIS). EIS, founded in 2007, is an on-going photography programme involving 43 cameras at 24 different glaciers around the world, each camera taking a photo for every hour of daylight in order to create time-lapse videos documenting the evolution of these glaciers. Since its release in 2012 the film has been screened in over 172 countries around the world, at the White House, and at a United Nations conference.[7]

The film – like *Ice and the Sky* – has two main narratives, one personal and one relating to the scientific recording of melting ice. In this case specifically the story of Balog's personal challenges on the one hand, and the story, as he puts it himself, that is 'in the ice' on the other. The notion that ice can tell its own story is a vital part of the film's rhetoric, as Balog and co-workers are presented as unbiased documentarists, catching on film things that are actually happening. The film is also built on the idea that the images are able to tell a story that words alone could not. Rather than rely on rational argumentation, *Chasing Ice* allows the ice to speak for itself by utilising powerful, emotive images of melting glaciers, together with sound and graphics that emphasise the message – a tactic that might be effective at dealing with those who distrust politicians, scientists or even statistical evidence. This is particularly relevant in the realm of climate science where, as we have discussed, the evidence often needs to be made visible. Communication scholar Jens E. Kjeldsen argues, in a paper on visual rhetoric, that 'pictorial representation has the ability of performing a sort of "thick description" which in an instant may provide a full sense of an actual situation', and furthermore that 'pictures are able to provide vivid presence, realism and immediacy in perception' (Kjeldsen 2013).

The images of the melting glaciers in *Chasing Ice* are indeed rich in information: the images show the size of the glacier, they indicate how much it is melting, and they specify the rate at which the changes are occurring. Removing the visual element weakens the argument, Kjeldsen asserts with good reason, reducing it to 'nothing more than "thin" propositions' (Kjeldsen 2013: 4).

This point can be made by taking a closer look at what must be described as both the visual and the argumentative climax of the film. We are shown footage of the Ilulissat glacier in Western Greenland, in what is thought to be the largest glacial calving event ever recorded on film. The footage shows almost unimaginably large pieces of ice being thrust hundreds of meters into the air, before falling back to the water, and drifting away. The full scene, lasting around 4 minutes, is an undeniably powerful experience. Being both beautiful and terrifying, clear parallels can be drawn to the romantic sublime, where the bystander simultaneously experiences the terror *and* the beauty of nature (Edmund 1998).

The majority of the time-lapses from the film are multi-annual compilations of images. The timescale is important to the accuracy of the film as it would be rather misleading to suggest that the Ilulissat event, lasting barely two hours, is representative of climate change on a global scale. It could be argued that the project (and, by extension, the film) can be considered a piece of science in its own right; the images collected for these time-lapses serve not only as visual evidence of climate change, but have been used by scientists to study the mechanics of glacial melting (Ahn and Box 2010). Balog, in his book *Ice: Portraits of Vanishing Glaciers* (2012), sums up the importance of time in relation to ice and photography, and in doing so also why the time-lapses are important to the film:

> We humans assume that we see the world in three dimensions. In fact, we also see in a fourth: time. Time is with us in every moment of everything observed. It is with us every time a camera clicks. In snapshot photography, or the street photography made famous by Henri Cartier-Bresson, that's obvious. But a different relationship with time is at work in EIS glacier photography. Time is an active character, visually explicit at times, implicit at others, constantly re-sculpting every molecule of frozen water. Everything you see on these pages will have changed substantially if not vanished entirely, by the time you hold this book.
>
> (Balog 2012)

The scenes, which include footage from glaciers in Iceland and Alaska, may not quite rival the Ilulissat segment but are nonetheless still fascinating and emotive in their own right.

However, let us return for a moment to the impressive glacier calving in order to better understand the intermedial rhetoric of the film, because it is characteristic for the film that despite the discourses on the magnificent abilities of the visual, the visual language is utterly reliant on non-visual aspects to succeed.

In the case of the Greenland glacier calving, this becomes obvious in the film's attempt to provide the spectator with a genuine understanding of the almost unfathomable scales involved. In order to provide a sense of scale, a graphically produced image of Manhattan is overlaid onto a time-lapse of the footage (Figure 8.3, Figure 8.4). The photographic visuality, in other words, is not enough to convey the truth about the scientific fact. Not only graphic design is needed to make the time-lapses

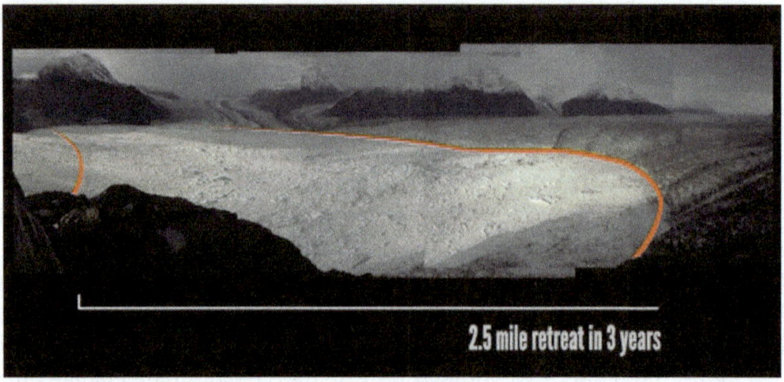

Figure 8.3 The intermedial rhetoric of *Chasing Ice* includes graphics, text and numbers.

Figure 8.4 The intermedial rhetoric of *Chasing Ice* includes graphics, text and numbers.

sufficiently striking, because at the same time that the images supplied for comparison of scale are provided, the creators of the film find it necessary to explain in a voice-over that the ice is, in fact, two to three times taller than the skyscrapers found in New York. Adding to the overall impact of the scene is the accompanying audio from the actual event. The graphics provide the two dimensions of length and breadth whereas the voice-over specifies the third dimension of height.

But there is more to this affectively striking scene, because the scene – as yet another intermedial layer – features both the cameramen's visceral, real-time reactions to what they are witnessing, as well as the thunderous sounds created by the glacier itself: these two sound-aspects, one of human voices, another of naturally produced noise, both recorded with technological equipment, provide a high level of authenticity to the scene. In other words, in spite of Orlowski and Balog's explicit tendencies in their films towards a monomedial reliance on

Figure 8.5 A dominant narrative in *Chasing Ice* is a man's (James Balog) battle to make climate change visible.

(photographic) visuality in order to convey something that may seem scarcely believable, in reality they rely on a complicated, heteromedial cinematic construction to make their point.

As alluded to previously, the second dominant narrative of the film is that of Balog's personal battle to set up the EIS (Figure 8.5). We are shown how he battles with faulty cameras, exploding batteries, adverse weather conditions, a chronic knee injury, and even an issue with foxes chewing through cables, in order to gather his evidence. Although unrelated to the central message of the film, this narrative is employed to demonstrate the human struggle involved in such a project. This narrative shares obvious similarities with the efforts of Lorius's research (relating to the *Bildungs* plot).

The general response to *Chasing Ice* has been positive, with reviewers suggesting that Balog and Orlowski succeed in their ambition to provide visual evidence of climate change: 'Offering a lesson both to filmmakers and climate-change deniers, *Chasing Ice* demonstrates how much more powerful it is to capture the real thing' (Jenkins 2016) and 'If any film can convert the climate-change sceptics, *Chasing Ice* would be it: here, seeing really is believing' (McCahill 2012). However, only seeing the raw footage of the EIS recording would not have made much sense to anyone and, without narrative schemas, the addition of editing, graphic editing and the careful use of sound elements, the film would undoubtedly never have had the well-deserved important success and, along with this, the impact that it did.

Conclusion: Seeing by way of man or media

The two films tell the stories of two men's battles against different hardships (nature itself (Figure 8.6), health and public ignorance), and against people's inability to 'see' – both visually and intellectually – what the two men have discovered, either by way of science or through the camera, or rather, through a combination of the two. For instance, the tagline on the DVD cover of *Ice and the Sky* is: 'One man's adventure would reveal Earth's greatest crisis'. *The Independent* compared Lorius with the adventurer Jack London, (MacNab 2015) and Mark Kermode in *The Guardian* even saw him as 'something of Moses in the aerial shots of the octogenarian surveying a receding icy ridge, or standing mournfully amid rising seas' (Kermode 2015). Balog has been described as a man on a solitary quest (*New York Times*), and the film about the EIS as 'primarily an adventure story about Balog and the challenges that he and his team had to overcome' (Genzlinger 2012). Accordingly, one can claim that turning the men into heroes comes with the cost of setting nature and climate change in the background. However, we also see some benefits in this approach. When discussing the visualisation of the Anthropocene, Nicholas Mirzoeff draws on the role visualisation has had in military history: 'Once the battlefield became too extensive and complex for any one person to physically see, the general's task was to visualise it by means of his imagination, supplied with ideas, images, and intuition from his staff and troops' (Mirzoeff 2009). The mark of the great man or the hero, according to Mirzoeff, was 'that he (always) could visualize history as it happened, unlike all other men' (Mirzoeff 2009: 206). We see these films as efforts to make visible something that people need to see, and in order to do that, they use a human figure at the centre of the stories.

Figure 8.6 James Balog's photographs are used as tools for making climate change visible.

Although it is problematic to make general claims about what documentary and cinema can or cannot do, based on these two examples alone, we have tried to put in *perspective* the often *foregrounded* (two visual metaphors!) question of the 'visualization of climate change', and we hope to have demonstrated that visuality is far from being the only meaning-making mediality of documentary.

Furthermore we have emphasised that the two films have similarities as well as differences. While both films are about man and ice, we see the two men as representing different roles. James Balog is the man with the camera, while Claude Lorius is the man with the microscope. *Ice and the Sky* can be seen as a portrait of the old man and the ice, and thus the film succeeds in giving climate science a face. *Chasing Ice* visualises *climate change*, but it is also in part a portrait of media technology and photography. *Ice and the Sky* offers insights into climate research and how scientists can make us see what is not discernible to the human eye by unveiling what is hidden underground. While *Ice and the Sky* can be said to offer the perspective of the microscope, the other film might be said to offer the larger picture on what visual media – cinema and photography – can do for climate communication. We have tried to stress that filmmakers, in reality, *combine* visual and verbal rhetoric as well as numerous other medial devices, thus achieving visual richness and semantic thickness supported by plot, music, and sound. Both films, and in particular *Chasing Ice*, become convincing by way of combining different media, images, sounds, words, numbers, scale and time. In the end, and here we agree with Kjeldsen, how we evaluate rhetorical reasoning boils down to criteria such as acceptability, relevance and sufficiency (Kjeldsen 2013).

The warming of the global climate is unequivocal, and it is imperative that efforts are made to combat the rising levels of CO_2. Communicating the science is vital to this and although we don't want to exaggerate the impact cinema can have on climate change communication, we do consider these films valuable contributions. In the end, the strongest impact of the films is their ability to make strong truth claims, and as such both transform form and content from scientific discourse to documentary, as well as expand it.

Notes

1. These are crucial questions to ask in cultural studies and media studies, in particular because the public gets most of their general information about science, including climate change, through the mass media. However, we will focus less on policy questions and more on formal discussions here. By not focusing on the question of possible political influence, this chapter differs from Cumming and Gjelsvik (2017) even though we borrow heavily from that article. See also Lowe (2006).

2. See for instance IPCC, (2013) and Cook et al. (2016).
3. 'Documentary Movies at the Box Office – Box Office Mojo: http://www.boxofficemojo.com/genres/chart/?id=documentary.htm (last accessed 16 October, 2016). It is second only to Michael Moore's controversial *Fahrenheit 9/11* as the best-selling documentary film to date.
4. 'Claude Lorius – Balzan Prize Climatology,': http://www.balzan.org/en/prizewinners/claude-lorius (last accessed 16 October, 2016).
5. For a discussion of the relation between music and cinema in a specific climate documentary, see Hart 2016.
6. And this is contrary for instance to the programme of Visual Culture Studies as formulated by W. J. T. Mitchell who reminds us 'that vision is itself invisible; that we cannot see what seeing is' (Mitchell 2002: 166).
7. Information from the project's own web page, 'Chasing Ice | Our Impact,' https://chasingice.com/ourimpact/ (last accessed 21 October, 2016).

9 Conclusion and Further Perspectives

The aim of this book has been both modest and immodest: we wished to suggest new ways of analysing narrative films for students and researchers, and hoped to tweak film theory a little bit in an intermedial direction. The reader may decide which of the two goals is the modest and which is the immodest one, but we have tried to do both.

In the Introduction, we presented a couple of questions that have guided the book and that represent its specific analytical objectives: What happens if we understand cinema as a mixed medium? How should one approach film analysis from an intermedial perspective? What thematic and formal traits will become clear when we look at film as a mixed mediality? In the rest of the introductory chapter, we tried to establish some of the theoretical foundations for rethinking cinema studies with an intermedial perspective. We have presented central theoretical discussions within intermedial studies as well as our own analytical three-step model, and we have selected seven intermedial questions that were exemplified in the eight narrative films that we worked with as our case studies.

When we presented our case studies, we were actually a little too modest in saying that 'their purpose is merely to exemplify our method'. We hope, on the contrary, to have offered substantial readings of the chosen films, so that our analyses may be of interest not only for methodological reasons, but also for scholars working with the genres or directors we have dealt with. We are well aware, however, that as a group of films, our cases are not at all comprehensive or representative, neither in terms of historical representation and geographical breadth nor cinematic genres. If we were to expand our project to include more different genres (while staying inside the same spatio-temporal realm) we would have liked to include both more commercial examples than we have worked on here, and more challenging experimental films. Genre movies such as *Star Wars: Rogue One* (Gareth Edwards 2016), *Wonder Woman* (Patty Jenkins 2017), *The Jungle book* (Jon Favreau 2016) or *Get Out* (Jordan Peele 2017), or art films such as *The Square* (Ruben Østlund 2017) or *The Exhibition* (Joanna Hogg 2013), as well as television series such as *Big Little Lies* (David E. Kelley and Jean-Marc Vallée 2017), *The Handmaid's Tale* (Bruce Miller 2017) or *Stranger Things*

(Matt and Joff Duffe 2016) would have been interesting to think about from an intermedial perspective. Working with shorter films, such as Don Hertzfeldt's animated short film *World of Tomorrow* (2015) or the Facebook horror film *Alexia* (Andrés Borges 2013), would have given us different possibilities and provided other ideas. We also certainly consider our approach relevant to the study of non-western films although none have been included here.

Looking back on the results of the theoretical framework and the methodological three-step model, we feel fairly confident that we are on the right track, both theoretically and analytically. Film studies, we think, do need to update all the fruitful 'proto-intermedial' insights from the earlier history of film and film criticism and stands to gain from incorporating central aspects of contemporary intermediality studies with these insights. The reluctance we have met from some film scholars towards intermediality – following the line that 'intermedial studies find out what film criticism has known all along' – will hopefully decrease. We are of course not claiming that intermedial studies can or should overtake or replace film theory, far from it, but what we do say is that the focus on the inherent mixedness of media, as well as some of the theoretical and analytical tools developed, in intermedial studies, may help clarify issues in film studies. One area where intermedial studies and film studies are already productively meeting is in adaptation studies, but other areas might benefit from such combined efforts as well: the study of sound is an obvious one.

Our focus on mediality as motif has demonstrated, we believe, a rich potential for further explorations, and the three steps of our analytical model – cataloguing, structuring, contextualising – work well as an analytical tool for research, but can also, we think, serve as a valuable aid in pedagogical situations. For students at most educational levels, and for critics, the three steps offer useful cognitive insights. The first step – cataloguing the presence of medialities – may feel rather mechanical or even banal. It does, however, bring home the awareness that lies at the bottom of media studies and intermedial studies, namely that medialities are constantly surrounding us and playing important roles in our lives. This basic condition tends to be very present, consciously or not, in narrative cinema, and the first step demonstrates this quite effectively. The second, structuring step may, with the maieutic help of some of the categories discussed or developed in intermedial theory like paragone, medium specificity, and others, help a student of film better organise the often rich presence of medialities. This step is not easy, but practising one's capacities in it will be rewarding in other fields of aesthetic analysis too; it develops cognitive skills such as ordering, choosing, and imagining a structured understanding of complex material. Finally, the third step's contextualising demands other efforts from the analysing mind, this time relating to aspects beyond the internal borders of the work itself, thus incorporating the film into larger historical, aesthetical, or perhaps psychological contexts.

But despite our optimism concerning the possible outcomes of our theoretical and analytical strategies, there are, needless to say, still improvements and additions to be made to what we have proposed here, which we, for now, will have to put on our imaginary film-intermediality wish list.

That list would include:

Thematic concentration: it might be productive to use the three-step model more instrumentally in investigating pre-established themes across cinematic genres (for instance gender, post-colonial questions, ecocritical issues) in order to avoid the possibly formalist bent of our analytical model.

Geographical and historical expansion: in terms of case studies, it would be fruitful to expand the analytical objects geographically (to reach beyond the Western canon in this book), but also to open up for historical considerations. Would the presence and function of a given set of medialities work the same way in early Asian film as in contemporary European film, for example? Probably not – and the differences would be worth investigating.

Generic expansion: it would be interesting to expand the analytical model to moving images that are not realistic-representative (say, American experimental film from the 1960s), or films that are less fictionalised and narrativised (Scandinavian instructional films related to public health, for instance). Would the suggested model work on these kinds of moving images? And if not, why? A first thesis would be, perhaps, that our model works well on films of a certain 'realistic' tendency, whereas our three-step model would be harder to apply to, for instance, avant-garde film. This leads to the next possible extension of our model:

An *intermedial expansion*: mediality as motif is a productive instrumentalisation of the abstract aspects of intermedial theory into a practical analytical methodology. But it comes with a methodological cost, namely that the analysis stays on a representational level often limited to the diegetic level of the films, the 'what' rather than the 'how', so to speak. This we could call the external mediality aspects. We have only very hastily discussed the technical media making cinema possible in the most practical but still very important ways: cameras, sound recording equipment, the sets relating to film production, but also all the technical aspects of the distribution and reception side of cinema. As mentioned above, our model, as it stands now, would be rather weak when confronted with, for instance a Stan Brakhage film from the 1960s or Thai director Apichatpong Weerasethakul's metaphysical films, where conventional representation, diegesis and narration is minimal or even absent. Or, more to the point concerning our case studies: what difference does it make to experience *Citizen Kane* in a movie theatre in 1941 as opposed to an art house cinema in the 1970s or on a computer screen in the twenty-first century? Generally, the importance of digital media and differences between screens and viewing modes could be further developed.

And last, but not least: *Pedagogical precision*: perhaps it would be interesting to specify even more the analytical model in terms of ages and educational levels? Should one version of the three-step model be offered to lower-grade students, while another, more complex one should be developed for graduate and post-graduate levels? What adjustments should be made?

But for now, we hope that our book will be seen as an opportunity to reconsider both some of the fundamental theoretical questions of film theory and a valuable guide to hands-on, practical suggestions on how to analyse narrative cinema. The book is aimed at higher-level students at universities and colleges, film scholars, and people simply interested in analysing and understanding film better. We hope the book will stimulate new, general visions of what cinema is and specific and exciting understandings of specific films.

Bibliography

Ahn, Y. and Jason E. Box (2010) 'Glacier velocities from time-lapse photos: technique development and first results from the Extreme Ice Survey (EIS) in Greenland,', *Journal of Glaciology*, 56 (198): 723–734.

Altman, R. (1980) *Cinema/Sound*, *Yale French Studies*, New Haven: Yale University Press.

Altman, R. (1992) *Sound Theory, Sound Practice*, *AFI film readers*, London: Routledge.

Anderson, B. (2011) 'Long Fall: The Most Famous 9/11 Photograph No One Has Seen', *Motherboard*.

Andrew, D. (2010) *What Cinema is! Bazin's Quest and its Charge*, Malden, MA: Wiley-Blackwell.

Andrew, J. D. (1976) *The Major Film Theories: An Introduction*, London: Oxford University Press.

Anonymous (2009) 'Maria Larssons evige øyeblikk', *Filmmagasinet*.

Arnheim, R. (1958) *Film as Art*, London: Faber and Faber.

Audi, A. (2016) 'Errol Morris on the Time He Filmed Donald Trump Missing the Point', *Literary Hub*.

Bakhtin, M. (1984) 'Problems of Dostoevsky's Poetics', edited and translated by Caryl Emerson, Introduction by Wayne C. Booth, Minneapolis, University of Minnesota Press.

Bal, M. (2010) *Of What One Cannot Speak: Doris Salcedo's Political Art*, Chicago: University of Chicago Press.

Balázs, B. (1924) *Der sichtbare mensch*, Wien, Leipzig: Deutsch-österreichischer Verlag.

Balog, J. (2012) *Ice: Portraits of Vanishing Glaciers*, New York: Rizzoli International Publications Inc.

Barker, J. M. (2004) *The Tactile Eye: Touch and the Cinematic Experience*, Berkeley: University of California Press.

Barthes, R. (1981) *Camera Lucida: Reflections on Photography*, New York: Hill and Wang.

Barthes, R. (1986) 'The Reality Effect' in *The Rustle of Language*, edited by Roland Barthes, 141–148, Oxford: Blackwell.

Bazin, A. (2009a) 'The Ontology of the Photographic Image', In *What is Cinema?*, edited by André Bazin, 3–12, Montréal: Caboose.

Bazin, A. (2009b) *What is Cinema?* Montréal: Caboose.

Bellour, R. (1975) 'The Unattainable Text' *Screen*, 16 (3): 19–27.

Bellour, R. (1987) 'The Pensive Spectator', *Wide Angle*, 9 (1): 6–10.

Bigelow, K. (2013) 'Kathryn Bigelow addresses "Zero Dark Thirty" torture criticism', *Los Angeles Times* <http://articles.latimes.com/2013/jan/15/entertainment/la-et-mn-0116-bigelow-zero-dark-thirty-20130116> (last accessed 5 October 2017).

Bojinski, S., M. Verstraete, T. C. Peterson, C. Richter, A. Simmons and M. Zemp (2014) 'The Concept of Essential Climate Variables in Support of Climate Research, Applications, and Policy', *Bulletin of the American Meteorological Society*, 95 (9): 1431–1443.

Bordwell, D. (1997) *On the History of Film Style*, Cambridge, MA: Harvard University Press.

Bordwell, D., J. Staiger, and K. Thompson (1985) *The Classical Hollywood Cinema: Film Style & Mode of Production to 1960*, New York: Columbia University Press.

Bordwell, D. and K. Thompson (2017) *Film Art: An Introduction*, 11th edition, New York: McGraw-Hill.

Bradshaw, P. (2014) 'Birdman (Or The Unexpected Virtue of Ignorance) review – a delirious, hallucinatory showbiz comedy', *The Guardian*, <https://www.theguardian.com/film/2014/dec/25/birdman-unexpected-virtue-of-ignorance-film-review> (last accessed 5 August 2017).

Brinch, S. (2006) 'Mellom stillstand og bevegelse – Pike med perleøredobb som filmatisk ekfrase', In *Estetiske teknologier 1700–2000*, edited by Gunnar Iversen, Oslo: Scandinavian Academic Press/Spartacus.

Brinch, S. (2013) 'Tracing the Original: The Film Invictus and "Based on a True Story" Adaptation', in *Adaptation Studies, New Challenges, New Directions*, edited by Jørgen Bruhn, Anne Gjelsvik and Eirik Frisvold Hanssen, London and New York, Bloomsbury.

Brody, R. (2014) '"Birdman" Never Achieves Flight', *The New Yorker*, 23 October, 2014.

Bruhn, J. (2010) 'Heteromediality', in *Media Borders, Multimodality and Intermediality*, 225–236, Springer.

Bruhn, J. (2016) *The Intermediality of Narrative Literature: Medialities Matter*. London: Palgrave Macmillan.

Bruhn, J., A. Gjelsvik, and E. F. Hanssen (2013) *Adaptation Studies: New Challenges, New Directions*, London and New York: Bloomsbury Academic.

Bruzzi, S. (2005) *New Documentary: A Critical Introduction*, London: Routledge.

Buncombe, A. (2016) 'Osama bin Laden: US Navy SEAL "kept unauthorised image of al-Qaeda leader's corpse"', *Independent* 20 January <http://www.independent.co.uk/news/people/osama-bin-laden-us-navy-seal-kept-unauthorised-image-of-al-qaeda-leaders-corpse-a6823156.html> (last accessed 3 January 2018).

Burgoyne, R. (2014) 'The Violated Body: Affective Experience and Somatic Intensity in Zero Dark Thirty', in *The Philosophy of War Films*, edited by David LaRocca, 247–60, Lexington: University Press of Kentucky.

Butler, J. (2009) *Frames of War: When is Life Grievable?* London, New York: Verso.

Bürger, P. (1984) *Theory and History of Literature, Volume 4: Theory of the Avant-Garde*, translated by M. Shaw, Manchester: Manchester University Press.

Campany, D. (2008) *Photography and Cinema*, London: Reaktion Books.

Carey, M. (2007) 'The History of Ice: How Glaciers Became an Endangered Species', *Environmental History*, 12 (3): 497–527.

Carringer, R. L. (1996) *The Making of Citizen Kane*, Berkeley: University of California Press.

Carroll, N. (1996) 'Medium Specificity Arguments and the Self-consciously Invented Arts: film, video, and photography', in *Theorizing the Moving Image*, edited by N. Carroll, 3–24, Cambridge: Cambridge University Press.

Carroll, N. (1998) 'Interpreting *Citizen Kane*', in *Interpreting the Moving Image*, Cambridge: Cambridge University Press.

Carver, R. (2007) 'Beginners', *The New Yorker*, 24 December.

Cavell, S. (1992) 'From the World Viewed', in *Film Theory and Criticism: Introductory Readings*, edited by G. Mast, M. Cohen and L. Braudy, 291–301, New York: Oxford University Press.

Chatman, S. (1980) 'What novels can do that films can't (and vice versa)', *Critical Inquiry* 7 (1): 121–140.

Chilton, M, (2015) 'Raymond Carver: the baleful star of Birdman', *The Telegraph*, 5 May <http://www.telegraph.co.uk/film/birdman/raymond-carver--the-baleful-star-of-birdman/> (last accessed 30 December 2017).

Chion, M. (1994) *Audio-vision: Sound on Screen*, translated by C. Gorbman, New York: Columbia University Press.

Clipper, L. J. (1981) 'Art and Nature in Welles' Xanadu', *Film Criticism* 5 (3): 12–20.

Clüver, C. (2007) 'Intermediality and interart studies', in Changing Borders: Contemporary Positions in Intermediality, edited by J. Arvidson, M. Askander, Bruhn, J. and H. Führer, Intermedia Studies Press: Lund, 19–38.

Coll, S. (2013) '"Disturbing" & "Misleading"', *The New York Review of Books*, 7 February.

Collin, R. (2015) 'Birdman: "spectacular"' *The Telegraph*, 22: 45, <http://www.telegraph.co.uk/films/2016/04/14/birdman-spectacular> (last accessed 5 May 2017).

Cook, J., N. Oreskes, P. T. Doran, W. R. L. Anderegg, B. Verheggen, E. W. Maibach, J. S. Carlton, S. Lewandowsky, A. G. Skuce, S. A. Green, D. Nuccitelli, P. Jacobs, R. Mark, B. Winkler, R. Painting, and K. Rice (2016) 'Consensus on Consensus: A Synthesis of Consensus Estimates on Human-caused Global Warming', *Environmental Research Letters*, 11 (4): 048002.

Corn, D. (2014) 'Senate torture report: No, bin Laden was not found because of CIA torture', *Mother Jones*, 9 December.

Corrigan, T., and P. Barry (2012) *The Film Experience: An Introduction*, 3rd edition, Basingstoke: Palgrave Macmillan.

Corner, J. (1995) *Television Form and Public Address*, London: Hodder.

Cumming, T., and A. Gjelsvik (2017) 'Icebreakers – Visionary Men and the Visualization of Climate Change', *Ekfrase* 7, 01–02: 21–35.

Dansgaard, W., H. B. Clausen, N. Gundestrup, C. U. Hammer, S. F. Johnsen, P. M. Kristinsdottir, and N. Reeh (1982) 'A New Greenland Deep Ice Core', *Science*, 218 (4579): 1273–1277.

Dargis, M. (2008) 'Two Friends, Two Novels, One Mailbox: Lives at the Speed of Ambition', Last Modified 16.5.2008, <http://www.nytimes.com/2008/05/16/movies/16repr.html?mcubz=1> (last accessed 22 September 2017).

Dargis, M. (2012) 'By Any Means Necessary: Jessica Chastain in "Zero Dark Thirty"', *The New York Times*, <http://www.nytimes.com/2012/12/18/movies/jessica-chastain-in-zero-dark-thirty.html> (last accessed 18 December 2017).

Dargis, M. (2014) "Birdman' Stars Michael Keaton and Emma Stone', *The New York Times*, <https://www.nytimes.com/2014/10/17/movies/birdman-stars-michael-keaton-and-emma-stone.html> (last accessed 17 October 2017).

Debruge, P. (2015) 'Film Review: "Louder Than Bombs"', *Variety*.

Degner, U., and N. C. Wolf (2010) *Der neue Wettstreit der Künste: Legitimation und Dominanz im Zeichen der Intermedialität*. Bielefeld: transcript.

Dunås, J. (2001) Apparaturbetraktelser. Metafilmiska aspekter på Jan Troells. Här har du ditt liv, Stockholm: Aura förlag.

Edgerton, G. (2013) 'Terror, Torture, Soldier, Spy', *Critical Studies in Television Online*.

Edmund, B. (1998) *A Philosophical Enquiry into the Origin of Our Ideas of the Sublime and Beautiful, Oxford World's Classics*, Oxford: Oxford University Press.

Elleström, L. (2010a) *Media Borders, Multimodality and Intermediality [Elektronisk resurs]*, Basingstoke: Palgrave Macmillan.

Elleström, L. (2010b) 'The Modalities of Media: A Model for Understanding Intermedial Relations', in *Media Borders, Multimodality and Intermediality*, 11–48. Springer.

Elleström, L. (2014) *Media Transformation: The Transfer of Media Characteristics Among Media*, Basingstoke: Palgrave Macmillan.

Elliott, K. (2003) *Rethinking the Novel/Film Debate*, Cambridge: Cambridge University Press.

Elsaesser, T. and M. Hagener (2009) *Film Theory: An Introduction Through the Senses*, London: Routledge.

Fish, S. (2010) 'Literary Criticism Comes to the Movies', *The New York Times*, <https://opinionator.blogs.nytimes.com/2010/10/04/literary-criticism-comes-to-the-movies/?_r=0> (last accessed 29 December 2017).

Finger, A. and D. Follett (eds) (2011) *The Aesthetics of the Total Artwork. On Borders and Fragments*, Baltimore: Johns Hopkins University Press.

French, P. (2009) 'Everlasting Moments', *The Guardian*, 24 September <https://www.theguardian.com/film/2009/may/24/everlasting-moments-film-review> (last accessed 5 August 2017).

French, P. (2011) '*Howl* review', *The Guardian*, 27 February <https://www.theguardian.com/film/2011/feb/27/howl-review-franco-ginsberg-hamm> (last accessed 30 December 2017).

Friedberg, A. (2006) *The Virtual Window: From Alberti to Microsoft*, Cambridge, MA: Massachusetts Institute of Technology Press.

Genette, G. (1980) *Narrative Discourse: An Essay in Method*, Ithaca, NY: Cornell University Press.

Genzlinger, N. (2012) '"Chasing Ice" Documents the Work of James Balog', *The New York Times*, 8 November <http://www.nytimes.com/2012/11/09/movies/chasing-ice-documents-the-work-of-james-balog.html> (last accessed 29 December 2017).

Geraghty, C. (2009) 'Foregrounding the media: Atonement (2007) as an Adaptation', 2 (2): 91–109.

Ghosh, A. (2016) *The Great Derangement: Climate Change and the Unthinkable*, London: University of Chicago Press.

Gianvito, J. (2006) *Andrei Tarkovsky: Interviews*, University Press of Mississippi.

Ginsberg, A. (1956) *Howl and Other Poems*, San Francisco: City Lights.

Gjelsvik, A. (2013) 'What Novels Can Tell That Movies Can't Show', In *Adaptation Studies: New Challenges, New Directions*, edited by J. Bruhn, A. Gjelsvik and E. F. Hanssen, 245–264, London: Bloomsbury.

Gottesman, R. (1971) *Focus on Citizen Kane*, Englewood Cliffs: Prentice Hall.

Gray, T. (2015) '"Birdman's' Times Square Scene: How They Did It", *Variety*, 14 January.

Gross, L. (2012) 'Some Ways into Zero Dark Thirty', *Film Comment* <https://www.filmcomment.com/blog/review-zero-dark-thirty-kathryn-bigelow> (last accessed 8 March 2018).

Gunning, T. (2008) 'What's the Point of an Index? Or Faking Photographs', in *Still/Moving: Between Cinema and Photography*, edited by K. Beckman and J. Ma, Durham, NC: Duke University Press.

Hanne, I. (2015) 'Claude Lorius, vétéran de l'Antarctique', *Libération*, 20 October <http://next.liberation.fr/cinema/2015/10/20/claude-lorius-veteran-de-l-antarctique_1407615> (last accessed 8 May 2017).

Hanssen, E. F. (2013a) 'The Hidden Spaces of the Theatre in George Cukor's A Double Life', *La Furina Umana*, (2): 49–54.

Hanssen, E. F. (2013b) 'Imaginary Museums, Material Refractions: André Bazin on Adaptation', in *Adaptation Studies: New Challenges, New Directions*, edited by J. Bruhn, A. Gjelsvik and E. F. Hanssen, 133–154, London: Bloomsbury.

Hart, H. (2016) 'Mozart on ice: Music as Anthropocene artifact in Expedition to the End of the World', in *Ekfrase, Nordisk tidsskrift for visuell kultur (Nordic Journal of Visual Culture)*, 1–2, Vol. 7, 39–49.

Harvey, G. (2010) 'The Two Raymond Carvers', *The New York Review of Books*, 27 May.

Hellsten, A. (2015) 'Louder Than Bombs Trier nosar elegant på livets stora teman', *Svenska Dagbladet.*

Hulme, M. (2015) 'Seeing Climate Change: For the few, for the many?', Human Side of Climate Change, Conference paper, 18 October.

Hutcheon, L. (2006) *A Theory of Adaptation*, London: Routledge.

Intergovernmental Panel on Climate Change (IPCC), Fifth Assessment Report (2014).

Isaacs, B. (2016) 'Reality Effects: The Ideology of the Long Take in the Cinema of Alfonso Cuarón', in *Post-cinema: Theorizing 21st-century Film*, edited by S. Denson and J. Leyda, 474–513, Falmer: REFRAME Books.

Jackson, M. (2015) 'Glaciers and Climate Change: Narratives of Ruined Futures', *Wiley Interdisciplinary Reviews: Climate Change* 6 (5): 479–492.

Jackson, T. E. (2008) 'Writing, Orality, Cinema: The "Story" of Citizen Kane', *Narrative* 16, (1): 29–45.

Jenkins, D. (2015) 'Ice and the Sky', *Little White Lies*, 11 December.

Jenkins, M. (2016) '"Chasing Ice" and Capturing Climate Change On Film', National Public Radio <https://www.npr.org/2012/11/08/164236520/chasing-ice-and-capturing-climate-change-on-film> (last accessed 29 December 2017).

Kaplan, E. A. (2015) *Climate Trauma: Foreseeing the Future in Dystopian Film and Fiction*, Rutgers University Press.

Kendall, P. (2015) 'Zero Dark Thirty: fact vs fiction', *The Telegraph*, 23 February <http://www.telegraph.co.uk/culture/film/film-news/9869992/Zero-Dark-Thirty-fact-vs-fiction.html> (last accessed 5 October 2017).

Kermode, M. (2015) 'Ice and the Sky review – awe-inspiring tribute to Claude Lorius', *The Guardian*, 13 December <https://www.theguardian.com/film/2015/dec/13/ice-and-sky-claude-lorius-scientist-global-warming> (last accessed 22 September 2016).

Kittler, F. A. (1999) *Gramophone, Film, Typewriter*, Friedrich A. Kittler; translated, with an introduction, by Geoffrey Winthrop-Young and Michael Wutz, Stanford: Stanford University Press.

Kjeldsen, J. E. (2013) 'Virtues of Visual Argumentation: How Pictures make the Importance and Strength of an Argument Salient', OSSA Conference Archive <http://scholar.uwindsor.ca/ossaarchive/OSSA10/papersandcommentaries/89> (last accessed 29 December 2017).

Kohn, E. (2015) 'Cannes Review: Joachim Trier's "Louder Than Bombs" is a Complex Family Drama Done Right', *Indiewire*.

Kozloff, S. (2000) *Overhearing Film Dialogue*, Berkeley: University of California Press.

Krauss, R. E. and M Broodthaers (2000) *A Voyage on the North Sea: Art in the Age of the Post-medium Condition*, New York: Thames & Hudson.

'Künstlerroman', Oxford University Press, <http://www.oxfordreference.com/view/10.1093/oi/authority.20110803100045770> (last accessed 9 September 2017).

Latour, B. (1999) *Pandora's Hope: Essays on the Reality of Science Studies*, Cambridge, MA: Harvard University Press.

Leitch, T. (2013) 'What Movies Want', in *Adaptation Studies: New Challenges, New Directions*, edited by J. Bruhn, A. Gjelsvik and E. F. Hanssen, London: Bloomsbury.

Leitch, T. M. (2009) *Film Adaptation and its Discontents: from Gone with the Wind to The Passion of the Christ.* Baltimore: Johns Hopkins University Press.

Lorius, C., J. Jouzel, C. Ritz, L. Merlivat, N. I. Barkov, Y. S. Korotkevich, and V. M. Kotlyakov (1985) 'A 150,000-year Climatic Record from Antarctic ice', *Nature* 316, (6029): 591–596.

Lowe, T. (2006) 'Is This Climate Porn? How Does Climate Change Communication Affect Our Perceptions and Behaviour?', Working paper <dcms2.lwec.ulcc.ac.uk/sites/default/files/wp98.pdf> (last accessed 30 December 2017).

Lund, H. (1992) *Text as Picture: Studies in the Literary Transformation of Pictures*, Lewiston: Edwin Mellen Press.

MacNab, G. (2015) 'Ice and the Sky, film review: Oscar-winner Luc Jacquet Returns', *The Independent*, 17 December <http://www.independent.co.uk/arts-entertainment/films/reviews/ice-and-the-sky-film-review-oscar-winner-luc-jacquet-returns-a6777201.html> (last accessed 22 September 2016).

Mälarstedt, K. (2011) *Jan Troell: regi, foto, klippning*, Stockholm: Norstedt.

Manovich, L. (1995) 'What is Digital Cinema?' <http://manovich.net/index.php/projects/what-is-digital-cinema> (last accessed 8 May 2017).

Manovich, L. (2001a) *The Language of New Media*, Cambridge, MA: MIT Press.

Manovich, L. (2001b) 'Post-media Aesthetics', <http://manovich.net/index.php/projects/post-media-aesthetics> (last accessed 8 May 2017).

Markiewicz, H. and U. Gabara (1987) '*Ut Pictura Poesis* . . . A History of the Topos and the Problem' in *New Literary History*, Vol. 18, No. 3, On Poetry, 535–558

Marks, L. (2000) 'The Skin of the Film', *Intercultural Cinema, Embodiment, and the Senses*: 162.

McCahill, M. (2012) 'Chasing Ice – review', *The Guardian*, 13 December <https://www.theguardian.com/film/2012/dec/13/chasing-ice-review> (last accessed 21 October 2016).

McCarthy, T. (2008) 'Review: 'Everlasting Moments', *Variety*, 3 September.

McDonald, S. (2004) 'Towards an Eco Cinema', *Interdisciplinary Studies in Literature and Environment*, Vol. 11, 2, 107–132.

McGilligan, P. (2015) *Young Orson: The Years of Luck and Genius on the Path to Citizen Kane*, New York: Harper.

Mirzoeff, N. (2006) 'Invisible Empire: Visual Culture, Embodied Spectacle, and Abu Ghraib', *Radical History Review*, (95): 21–44.

Mirzoeff, N. (2009) *An Introduction to Visual Culture*, 2nd edition, London: Routledge.

Mitchell, W. T. J. (2011) *Cloning Terror: The War of Images, 9/11 to the Present*, Chicago: University of Chicago Press.

Mitchell, W. J. T. (2002) 'Showing Seeing: A Critique of Visual Culture', *Journal of visual culture*, 1 (2): 165–181.

Mitchell, W. J. T. (2005) 'There are no visual media', *Journal of visual culture*, 4 (2): 257–266.

Mitchell, W. J. T, and M. B. N. Hansen (2010) *Critical terms for media studies*, Chicago and London: University of Chicago Press.

Morgan, B. and N. J. Peters (eds) (2006), Howl on Trial: The Battle for Free Expression, San Francisco: City Lights.

Mortensen, M. (2012) *Kampen om ansigtet: fotografi og identifikation*. Kbh.: Museum Tusculanum.

Morton, T. (2016) *Dark Ecology: For a Logic of Future Coexistence*, New York; Chichester: Columbia University Press.

Moore, M. (2017) 'In Defense of Zero Dark Thirty', Facebook post 24 January <https://www.facebook.com/mmflint/posts/10151199285611857> (last accessed 4 January 2018).

Mulvey, L. (1992) *Citizen Kane*, London: British Film Institute Publishing.

Mulvey, L. (2006) *Death 24x a Second: Stillness and the Moving Image*, London: Reaktion Books.

Musser, C. (2015) 'Trauma, Truth and the Enviromental Documentary', in *Eco-trauma Cinema*, Abingdon: Routledge.

Naremore, J. (2004) *Orson Welles's Citizen Kane: A Casebook*, New York: Oxford University Press.

Narine, A. (2015) *Eco-trauma Cinema*. Vol. 33, Routledge advances in film studies, New York: Routledge.

Nichols, B. (1991) *Representing the Real. Issues and Concepts in Documentary*. Bloomington: Indiana University Press.

Nixon, R. (2011) *Slow Violence and the Environmentalism of the Poor*, Cambridge, MA: Harvard University Press.

Nordic Film Council (2016) Winner of the Nordic Council Film Prize 2016 <http://www.norden.org/en/nordic-council/nordic-council-prizes/nordisk-raads-filmpris-1/winner-of-the-nordic-council-film-prize-2016> (last accessed 22 July 2017).

Orlove, B., E. Wiegandt and B, H, Luckman (2008) 'The Place of Glaciers in Natural and Cultural Landscape', in *Darkening Peaks, Glacier Retreat, Science and Society*, Berkeley: University of California Press.

Paech, J. (2011) 'The intermediality of film', *Acta Universitatis Sapientiae, Film and Media Studies*, (4): 7–21.

Peters, J. D. (1999) *Speaking into the Air: A History of the Idea of Communication*, Chicago: University of Chicago Press.

Pethő, Á. (2011) *Cinema and Intermediality: The Passion for the In-between*, Newcastle upon Tyne: Cambridge Scholars Publishing.

Pethő, Á. (2013) 'The Vertigo of the Single Image: From the Classic Narrative "Glitch" to the Post-Cinematic Adaptations of Paintings', *Acta Universitatis Sapientiae, Film and Media Studies*, (06): 65–90.

Petit, J. R., J. Jouzel, D. Raynaud, N. I. Barkov, J. M. Barnola, I. Basile, M. Bender, J. Chappellaz, M. Davis, G. Delaygue, M. Delmotte, V. M. Kotlyakov, M. Legrand, V. Y. Lipenkov, C. Lorius, L. Pépin, C. Ritz, E. Saltzman, and M. Stievenard (1999) 'Climate and atmospheric history of the past 420,000 years from the Vostok ice core, Antarctica', *Nature* 399 (6735): 429–436.

Prince, M. J. (2012) "Howl: A Novel Graphic: Authencity and Irony in Eric Drooker's Adaptation of Allen Ginsberg's "Howl"", SCAN 9, June <http://scan.net.au/scan/journal/display.php?journal_id=164> (last accessed January 2018).

Rajewsky, I. O. (2014) 'Intermedialität, Remediation, Multimedia', In *Handbuch Medienwissenschaft*, edited by J. Schröter, 197–206, Stuttgart/Weimar: Metzler.

Renov, M. (1993) *Theorizing documentary*, New York and London: Routledge.

Roddick, N. (2015) 'Louder Than Bombs – first look', *Sight & Sound.* Accessed 09/05/2017. <http://www.bfi.org.uk/news-opinion/sight-sound-magazine/reviews-recommendations/cannes-2015-louder-than-bombs> (last accessed 9 May 2017).

Rodowick, D. N. (2007) *The Virtual Life of Film*, Cambridge, MA and London: Harvard University Press.

Rudiak-Gould, P. (2013) '"We Have Seen It with Our Own Eyes": Why We Disagree about Climate Change Visibility', *WEATHER, CLIMATE, AND SOCIETY* 5.

Røssaak, E. (2008) *Negotiating Immobility: The Moving Image and the Arts in Andy & Larry Wachowski's The Matrix, Ken Jacobs's Tom, Tom, The Piper's Son, and Bill Viola's The Passions*, Ph.D. thesis, Unipub AS, Oslo, Acta Humaniora, no. 348.

Rust, S., S. Monani, S. Cubitt (2013) *Ecocinema. Theory and Practice*, New York: Routledge.

Sandberg, M. (2017) '*Mad Men*'s Serially Falling Man', *The Velvet Light Trap*, Vol. 79, No. 1, 4–20, *Project MUSE*, muse.jhu.edu/article/648147.

Salmon, P. (2006) '"THE PEOPLE WILL THINK . . . WHAT I TELL THEM TO THINK": Orson Welles and the Trailer for Citizen Kane', *Revue canadienne d'études cinématographiques/Canadian Journal of Film Studies*, 96–113.

Schröter, J. (2010) "The Politics of Intermediality – New and Novelty in Contemporary Media Cultures." *Acta Univ. Sapientia, Film and Media Studies*, 2, 107–124.

Scott, A. O. (2010) 'Leaping off the Page, a Beatnik's Poetic Rant', *The New York Times* <http://movies.nytimes.com/2010/09/24/movies/24howl.html?pagewanted=all> (last accessed 8 February 2012).

Scranton, R. (2015) *Learning to Die in the Anthropocene: Reflections on the End of a Civilization*, San Francisco: City Lights.

Selås, J. (2015) 'Filmanmeldelse: «Louder Than Bombs»', *VG*. 17 May http://www.vg.no/rampelys/film/filmanmeldelser/filmanmeldelse-louder-than-bombs/a/23454101> (last accessed 9 May 2017).

Selås, J. (2010) 'Gulnet, gammeldags, glimrende! ', *VG*. 16 October, <http://www.vg.no/film/artikkel.php?artid=538078> (last accessed 8 May 2017).

Sødtholt, D. (2016) "*Louder Than Bombs*: Joachim Trier's play on perspective", *Montages*, 16 January <http://montagesmagazine.com/2016/01/louder-than-bombs-joachim-triers-play-on-perspective> (last accessed 30 December 2017).

Sontag, S. (1966) *Against Interpretation, and Other Essays*, New York: Farrar.

Sontag, S. (1977) *On Photography*, New York: Farrar, Straus and Giroux.

Stanitzek, G. and N. Aplevich (2009) 'Reading the Title Sequence (Vorspann, Générique)', *Cinema Journal*, 48 (4): 44–58.

Sternberg, M. (1999) 'The "Laokoon" Today: Interart Relations, Modern Projects and Projections' in *Poetics Today*, Vol 20, 291–379.

Sterritt, D. (2011) 'Howl', *Journal of American History*, 98 (1): 298–301.

Sørenssen, B. (2001) *Å fange virkeligheten: dokumentarfilmens århundre*, Oslo: Universitetsforlaget.

Thomson, D. (2016) 'How Louder Than Bombs Dares to Discuss some of our Stickiest Relationships', *The Guardian*, <https://www.theguardian.com/film/filmblog/2016/apr/21/why-louder-than-bombs-dares-to-discuss-stickiest-family-relationships> (last accessed 9 May 2017).

Tornborg, E. (2014) 'What Literature can make us see: Poetry, intermediality, mental imagery', Doctoral Thesis, Department of Film and Literature, Linnaeus University.

Trier, J. (2016) 'Making movies takes something out of you every time', edited by D. Jenkins, *Little White Lies*.

Trier, J. (2017) 'Joachim Trier in a telephone conversation with Anne Gjelsvik', 1 September.

Trueman, M. (2015) 'Birdman: The Best Film About Theatre Ever Made?', *The Guardian*, 1 July <https://www.theguardian.com/stage/2015/jan/07/birdman-best-film-about-theatre-ever-made> (last accessed 5 August 2017).

Ulfsäter-Troell, A. (2007) *Att människan levde en släktkronika: Maria Larssons eviga ögonblick*. Mariehamn: PQR-Kultur.

Weber, E., I. Bauman, Eliasson, and Olafur (2014) 'Can Art Inspire Climate Change Action? An Ice Installation Aims To Do Just That', *The Guardian*, 23 October <https://www.theguardian.com/sustainable-business/2014/oct/23/climate-change-ice-watch-installation-art-greenland-copenhagen-ipcc> (last accessed 15 September 2015).

The White House (2013) 'Remarks by the President at the National Defense University', 23 April <https://obamawhitehouse.archives.gov/the-press-office/2013/05/23/remarks-president-national-defense-university> (last accessed 3 January 2018).

Winston, B. (2013) *The Documentary Film Book, A BFI Book*, Basingstoke and London: Palgrave Macmillan/BFI.

Wolf, W. (2005) 'Intermediality', In *Routledge Encyclopedia of Narrative Theory*, edited by D. Herman, M. Jahn and M.-L. Ryan, 252–256, London and New York: Routledge.

Wolf, W. (2008) 'The Relevance of Mediality and Intermediality to Academic Studies of English Literature', In *Medality/Intermediality*, edited by A. Fischer, M. Heusser and A. H. Jucker, 15–43, Tübingen: Gunter Narr Verlag.

Wolf, W. (2011) '(Inter) mediality and the Study of Literature', *CLCWeb: Comparative Literature and Culture* 13 (3): 2.

Zemp, M., H. Frey, I. Gärtner-Roer, S. U. Nussbaumer, M. Hoelzle, F. Paul, W. Haeberli, F. Denzinger, A. P. Ahlstrøm, B. Anderson, S. Bajracharya, C. Baroni, L. N. Braun, B. E. Cáceres, G. Casassa, G. Cobos, L. R. Dávila, H. Delgado Granados, M. N. Demuth, L. Espizua, A. Fischer, K. Fujita, B. Gadek, A. Ghazanfar, J. O. Hagen, P. Holmlund, N. Karimi, Z. Li, M. Pelto, P. Pitte, V. V. Popovnin, C. A. Portocarrero, R. Prinz, C. V. Sangewar, I. Severskiy, O. Sigurðsson, A. Soruco, R. Usubaliev and C. Vincent (2015) 'Historically Unprecedented Global Glacier Decline in the Early 21st Century', *Journal of Glaciology*, 61 (228): 745–762. doi: 10.3189/2015JoG15J017.

Žižek, S. (2013) 'Zero Dark Thirty: Hollywood's Gift to American Power', *The Guardian*, 25 January <https://www.theguardian.com/commentisfree/2013/jan/25/zero-dark-thirty-normalises-torture-unjustifiable> (last accessed 5 October 2017).

Film references

8½, directed by Federico Fellini, Italy: Cinecittà Studio, 1963.
60 Minutes II: Inside Abu Ghraib, USA: CBS, 2004.
Alexia, directed by Andrés Borges, Argentina: Estrella Infernal, 2013.
Amores Perros, directed by Alejandro G. Iñárritu, Mexico: Altavista Films, 2000.
Arven, directed by Anja Breien, Norway: Norsk Film, 1979.
Arrival, directed by Denis Villeneuve, USA: Paramount Pictures, 2016.
Assassins Creed, directed by Justin Kurzel, UK: Regency Enterprises, 2016.
Atonement, directed by Ian Wright, UK/France/USA: Universal Pictures, 2007.
The Avengers, directed by Joss Whedon, USA: Marvel Studio, 2012.
Babel, directed by Alejandro G. Iñárritu, USA: Paramount Pictures, 2012.
Batman, directed by Tim Burton, USA: Warner Brothers, 1989.
Batman Begins, directed by Christopher Nolan, USA: Warner Brothers, 2005.
Batman Returns, directed by Tim Burton, USA: Warner Brothers, 1992.
Big Little Lies, created by David E. Kelley and directed by Jean-Marc Vallée, USA: Blossom Films, 2017.
Birdman, directed by Alejandro G. Iñárritu, USA: New Regency Films, 2014.
Blind, directed by Eskil Vogt, Norway: Lemming Film & Motlys, 2014.
Celluloid Closet, directed by Rob Epstein and Jeffrey Friedman, USA: Sony Picture Classics, 1995.
Chasing Ice, directed by Jeff Orlowski, USA: Exposure, 2012.
Children of Men, directed by Alfonso Cuarón, USA: Universal Pictures, 2006.
The Dark Knight, directed by Christopher Nolan, USA: Warner Brothers, 2008.
The Dark Knight Rises, directed by Christopher Nolan, USA: Warner Brothers, 2012.
The Day After Tomorrow, directed by Roland Emmerich, USA: Twentieth Century Fox, 2004.
A Double Life, directed by George Cukor, USA: Kanin Production, 1947.
Drone, directed by Tonje Hessen Schei, Norway: Filmmer Film, 2014.
Elephant, directed by Gus van Sant, USA: HBO Films, 2003.
En frusen dröm, directed by Jan Troell, Sweden: Athenafilm, 1997.
Everlasting Moments (Maria Larssons eviga ögonblick), directed by Jan Troell, Sweden/Denmark: Blind Spot Pictures Oy, 2009.
Exhibition, directed by Joanna Hogg, United Kingdom: Wild Horse Film Company et al., 2013.
Eye in the Sky, directed by Gavin Hood, UK: Raindog Films, 2015.
Get Out, directed by Jordan Peele, USA: Blumhouse Productions, 2017.
Girl with a Pearl Earring, directed by Peter Webber, UK: Archer Street Productions, 2003.

Goodfellas, directed by Martin Scorsese, USA: Warner Brothers, 1990.
Good Kill, directed by Andrew Nicol, USA: Voltage Pictures, 2014.
Gravity, directed by Alfonso Cuarón, UK/USA: Warner Brothers, 2013.
Hamsun, directed by Jan Troell, Sweden/Norway/Denmark: Nordisk Film et al., 1996.
The Handmaid's Tale, created by Bruce Miller, USA: MGM Television, 2017.
The Hobbit (Trilogy), directed by Peter Jackson, USA/New Zealand: New Line Cinema, 2012–2014.
Homeland, created by Howard Gordan and Alex Gansa, USA: Teakwood Lane Productions, 2011–.
Howl, directed by Rob Epstein and Jeffrey Friedman, USA: Werc Werk Works, 2010.
The Hurt Locker, directed by Kathryn Bigelow, USA: Voltage Pictures, 2008.
Ice Age, directed by Chris Wedge and Carlos Saldanha, USA: 20th Century Fox Film, 2002.
Ice and the Sky, directed by Luc Jaquet, France: Pathé, 2015.
The Ice Storm, directed by Ang Lee, USA: Good Machine, 1997.
Il Capitano, directed by Jan Troell, Sweden: Pan Film 1991.
An Inconvenient Truth, directed by David Guggenheim, USA: Lawrence Bender Productions, 2006.
Ingenjör Andrées luftfärd, directed by Jan Troell, Sweden: Adnorsk, 1982.
Interstellar, directed by Christopher Nolan, USA: Paramount Pictures/Warner Brothers, 2015.
Iron Man, directed by Jon Favreau, USA: Paramount Pictures, 2008.
La Jetée, directed by Chris Marker, France: Argos Film, 1962.
The Jungle Book, directed Jon Favreau, USA: Disney et al., 2016.
Louder Than Bombs, directed by Joachim Trier, Norway: Motlys, 2015.
Le Mépris, directed by Jean-Luc Godard, France: Les Films Concordia, 1963.
Life of Pi, directed by Ang Lee, USA: Fox 2000 pictures, 2012.
The Lord of the Rings (Trilogy), directed by Peter Jackson, USA/New Zealand: New Line Cinema, 2001–2003.
Manchester by the Sea, directed by Kenneth Lonergran, USA, Amazon Studios, 2016.
March of the Penguins, directed by Luc Jacquet, France: National Geographic Films, 2005.
The Matrix, directed by Lilly Wachowski and Lana Wachowski, USA: Warner Brothers, 1999.
The Mill and the Cross, directed by Lech Majewski, Poland: Telewizja Polska (TVP), 2011.
Mr. Turner, directed by Mike Leigh, UK: Film4, 2014.
My Dinner with Andre, directed by Louis Malle, USA: Saga Productions Inc., 1981.
Nybyggarna, directed by Jan Troell, Sweden: Svensk Filmindustri, 1972.
Närvarande, directed by Jan Troell, Sweden: Athenafilm, 2003.
Opening Night, directed by John Cassavettes, USA: Faces Distribution, 1977.
Ordinary People, directed by Robert Redford, USA: Paramount Pictures, 1980.
Opera, directed by Dario Argento, Italy: ADC Films, 1987.
Oslo, August 31st, directed by Joachim Trier, Norway: Motlys, 2011.
Persepolis, directed by Marjane Satrapi, and Vincent Paronnaud, France: 2.4.7. Films, 2007.

Pierrot Le Fou, directed by Jean-Luc Godard, France: Films Georges de Beauregard, 1965.
The Revenant, directed by Alejandro G. Iñárritu, USA: Regency Enterprises, 2015.
Reprise, directed by Joachim Trier, Norway: 4½ Film, 2006.
Rope, directed by Alfred Hitchcock, USA: Warner Brothers, 1948.
Sagolandet, directed by Jan Troell, Sweden: Bold Productions, 1988.
Sherlock, created by Mark Gatiss and Steven Moffat, UK: Hartswood Films, 2010–2016.
Sherlock Holmes, directed by Guy Ritchie, USA: Warner Brothers, 2009.
Snowpiercer, directed by Bong Jon-hoo, South Korea/Czech Republic: Moho Film, 2013.
The Square, directed by Ruben Østlund, Sweden: Plattform Produktion et al., 2017.
Star Wars: Rogue One, directed by Gareth Edwards, USA: Lucas Film, 2016.
Stories We Tell, directed by Sarah Polley, Canada: National Film Board of Canada, 2012.
Stranger Things, created by Matt and Joff Duffe, USA: 21 Laps Entertainment Productions and Monkey Massacre, 2016.
The Sweet Hereafter, directed by Atom Egoyan, Norway: Alliance Communications Corporation, 1997.
Så vit som en snö, directed by Jan Troell, Sweden: Film i Skåne, Nordisk Film, SVT, Svensk Filmindustri, 2001.
Times of Harvey Milk, directed by Rob Epstein, USA: Black Sands Production, 1984.
Tom, the Piper's Son, directed by Ken Jacobs, USA, 1969.
Tristram Shandy: A Cock and Bull Story, directed by Michael Winterbottom, UK: BBC Films, 2005.
United 93, directed by Paul Greengrass, USA: Universal Pictures, 2006.
Utvandrarna, directed by Jan Troell, Sweden: Svensk Filmindustri, 1971.
Waltz with Bahir, directed by Ari Folman, Israel, Bridgit Folman Film Gang/Les Films d'Ici/Razor Film Produktion GmbH, 2008.
We Need to Talk About Kevin, directed by Lynne Ramsay, UK/ USA: BBC Films, 2011.
Wings of Desire, directed by Wim Wenders, West Germany: Road Movies Filmproduktion, 1987.
Wonder Woman, directed by Patty Jenkins, USA: Warner Brothers, 2017.
World of Tomorrow, directed by Don Hertzfeldt, USA: Bitter Film Production, 2015.
X-Men, directed by Bryan Singer, USA: Twentieth Century Fox Film, 2000.
Zero Dark Thirty, directed by Kathryn Bigelow, USA: Columbia Pictures, 2012.

Index